Thank God for Boll Weevils

To Joanne,

May God Bless you + every step
you take in this life!

Rhett Barr

Tiger Iron Press
Savannah, Georgia

Thank God for Boll Weevils

By

Rhett Barbaree

Tiger Iron Press

Cover design by Julianne Gleaton, www.juliannedesign.com

Book design by E. Michael Staman, Mike.Staman@TigerIronPress.com

Library of Congress Cataloging-in-Publication Data
Thank God for Boll Weevils / Rhett Barbaree
ISBN 978-0-9851745-2-1

Search by: 1. Southern fiction. 2. Rhett Barbaree. 3. Alabama. 4. Enterprise, Al. 5. Boll Weevil. 6. George Washington Carver. 7. Cotton. 8. Cotton production. 9. Southern peanut production.

First Edition: 2012

Printed in the United States of America

The story you are about to read is a fictionalized version based upon fact, though some might insist that if it did not happen this way it very well could have.

Dedication

This book is dedicated to the nine people (including the eight students of Enterprise High School in Alabama) who lost their lives during the tornado of 2007. God sometimes allows a tragedy in our lives to change the road we are on. The difference is the ones you now walk are all paved with gold.

and

To my father, who walks these same Heavenly streets.

Your road led through the sea, your pathway through the mighty waters, a pathway no one knew was there.

Psalms 77:19

Prologue

Pastor Seth always said we should make a Big Thank You to God List, and we should keep it going for the rest of our lives.

"When things ain't goin your way and you're feelin down, you can pull that list out from wherever you keep it and remind yourself that Gawd is in the blessin business!" he'd shout. "And then after you do that, I want you to take those lips of yorn and instead of poor mouthin about the things you may be a facin at the time, I want you to start praisin Him for how he will turn all of it into somethin good. 'Cause folks, I want you to understand somethin, and I want you to let it sink in real good: Gawd allows things to happen for a reason. It might not make no sense to begin with, and it might be the most painful and aggravatin thing you've ever faced in your life, but you remember this: He knows about ever situation before you ever go through it; you just gotta learn to trust Him. Then one day, I promise, when you're older and you're lookin back on your life, you'll not only understand a little better why things happened the way they did, but you'll begin liftin up those things you wanted to curse so bad, and you'll lift 'em up towards Heaven and start thankin Him for 'em."

Chapter 1

Janie

It was the year 1905 when Daddy Jack died. He was buried in December, right next to where Granny May had been resting for almost twelve years. Though I was but ten when he passed, his death was frozen into my mind by the same frosty winds that had hung icicles from our rooftop just the night before. Even Ol' General Bob, who loved to drown folks out with his Yankee-fighting stories, confessed it was cold that day, and he was the sort who tried to one-up most anything being said.

At the funeral, Pastor Seth preached a good while about how the departed had gotten to cross over. But being young I rarely considered such things. I just figured I'd stay where I was in life, or at least hold on to it as long as I could, hoping each new day would offer as much fun as the last one had.

Where I grew up was a small town in south Alabama called Enterprise, and I don't think God could have ever put me in a better place. There was hardly a day went by where a whole handful of us weren't making up games, such as Ghost in the Bushes or Headless Horseman, both of which made us holler out so loud, we could have woke the dead. And you couldn't put a good dose of devilment past anyone of us either. It all seemed harmless at the time, and most of the folks we visited it on never seemed to lose any sleep over what we did to them, anyway. There were exceptions though, and one of them was General Bob himself. The poor soul, he never caught on to the things we tortured him with. Many a time, half a dozen or so of us would creep up real quiet around his house, hoping to catch him napping with the windows open. Then we'd take a stick and rap it upside his house just to see what orders he'd holler out to the long-departed soldiers who had once been under his command. We learned lots of new words and phrases every time we did this, most of which we knew not to repeat. Course we always told Daddy what General Bob would say, and my Daddy, being a prankster himself, would usually laugh about it 'till he almost fainted. When Mama would get onto us for such foolishness, Daddy would say what we did to General Bob was payback for him taking up so much of our time with his war stories.

We got the idea from the Sundays the general would doze off in church. Every now and then, someone would drop a hymnal and General Bob would yell out with curses or cover himself like a cannonball was whistling over his head. It got to the point where someone would drop one on purpose just to see General Bob's reaction. Pastor Seth caught on after awhile to what we were doing and banned the young folks from holding a hymnal.

The thing that broke us from harassing General Bob though, was the time I dared my brother Jessup to crawl up on his porch while he snored and run a piece of cloth through his belt loop and then tie it to the back of the rocking chair he was sitting in. Jess eased up on the porch like a cat stalking a bird and carefully ran the cloth through a loop and then knotted it around a spindle on the chair. He then eased back down, picked up an old bugle someone had given him and blew it as hard as he could.

Ol' Bob woke up a hollering, then rocked forward to stand up and fell over face first, hitting his head on the floor boards of the porch. We had just killed 'em dead!

Now, it was only a matter of time before Miss Firtie, his live-in help, would have Sheriff Tyril and his tracking hounds out searching for the culprits. Jess and I ran from there as fast as we could, then debated back and forth in pure fear as to what we should do. Finally, we came to the conclusion that we had to go and tell Daddy and suffer the consequences, even if that meant being hung for murder. We were headed that way when it dawned on me that we should cut across Mr. Dooley's place and peep through the bushes to see if Miss Firtie had found General Bob yet. Being very quiet, Jess and I parted the bushes and when we did our bodies went as limp as licorice on a hot day.

There he sat in his chair, Miss Firtie holding an ice rag to his head and asking him how many fingers she was holding up.

"Two!" he yelled and then demanded she get him his whiskey she'd hidden some weeks before.

Praise God! He was still alive! And at that very moment, Jess and I both experienced enough relief for a lifetime. We knew there would be no gallows for us now – something the town's people would have turned out by the hundreds to see. But most of all we knew God had done us a huge favor that day – one of which I was most grateful for, and kept at the top of my – Big Thank You to God List – for a long time.

As far as Daddy Jack's funeral goes, his casket was brought to Aunt Lois's house the night before, where it was laid out in a room she called "the parlor."

"Her house is so dadgum big," Daddy would say, "that's she's bound to have young'uns in there she ain't never met before."

Aunt Lois's house was the showplace of Enterprise, with a large manicured lawn and fancy doodads scattered every whichaway to set off the picket fence around the whole yard. The night before Daddy Jack's funeral, Jess and me and several cousins were running around the property hollering and screaming. Daddy, who was usually mild tempered, came quick stepping up to us and said in a low, angry growl, "Daddy Jack is layin up yonder in that front room dead," he said pointing toward the house, "and you and Jess is runnin around here like a bunch of wild Injuns. Here; blow your nose," he said while taking his handkerchief out. Now, to this very day I am still at a loss as to why Daddy got so mad about the situation. First off, Daddy Jack never paid us much attention anyway. He was like a dog with no tail: You never knew if he was glad to see you or not. The other thing was, he was dead now, and I don't reckon he could have heard us hollering, especially as far away from the house as we were.

To be fair about it, though, there were times he actually did talk to us. It was usually in his garden, something he was proud to show off. On those occasions we would follow him around his patch, all the while him pointing out what different things he'd be growing when the season came.

"Janie," he said, spitting his tobacco, "these here are my turnips. I planted 'em some weeks ago and you and Jess can take a mess of 'em home when ya start to leave."

During the summer, he'd show us his squash and cucumbers, okra and watermelons, and an abundance of peas, corn, butter beans, and cantaloupe, all planted with "my secret seeds," he'd say. We believed him, too, for every Fourth of July when Coffee County had its huge celebration, Daddy Jack would have several blue ribbons placed on his sample baskets. The other contestants being disappointed would stand, shake their heads from side to side, and then slowly pack up their goods and leave. At the end of every harvest, Daddy Jack would carefully examine what he gathered, placing some of the very best aside for the next year's growing seeds. When he was finally laid to rest, I remember Pastor Seth saying something about sowing and reaping, and how appropriate those words were for him.

My mother, who was Daddy Jack's only daughter and last surviving child, was quiet for some time after he passed. As I got older, I would often look back on that time in Mama's life and realize the unspoken words she had were those of regret and loss: regret for the affections her daddy had never shown her as a child and now that he had passed, the loss that he would never have the chance to do so. During that dark storm in her life, Jess and I figured the best thing for us to do was to be as cheerful as possible and not fight over the chores. We managed our part, but after awhile, we began wondering if our good behavior was really making any difference, and worried that no matter what we did, Mama would never smile or laugh again.

Then one Sunday when Pastor Seth had been invited over to our house to eat lunch after church services, Mama finally let go of her feelings. Just as we were all being seated, Jess walked up to the table and placed three corn cobs, two red ones and one white one, in front of Pastor Seth. "Preacher," Jess said, trying to sound like he was grown, "when you go to the privy, you can take these with ya. Use the two reds ones first, then check yourself with the white one."

I absolutely froze in horror of what my brother had just done, partly from embarrassment and partly because I knew this was probably to be his last day on this earth. I looked over at Mama, who had heard every word. She put her head down a little, placing it in her hands, and began to shake it from side to side. Then her whole body started to shake, just a little at first, but steadily more pronounced as her shoulders quivered and she rocked back and forth a couple of times. Then she took her fist from one hand and began slightly beating it on the table. Daddy, fully knowing what Mama had been going through the past month, reached over with one arm to gently help her up and away from the table. It was then that Mama could no longer hold it in. Her fist came down hard and with it, such a howl of laughter that it startled us all. Her eyes were wet with tears and her face was red from the lack of air she couldn't breathe. I had never seen her laugh so hard in my entire life, and it was shocking!

Then, after she finally seemed to find an end to it, Pastor Seth, who had been watching Mama with a very queer look on his face, reached over, took the three cobs and put them in his shirt pocket, saying " I hope me takin these won't put y'all short. If it does, y'all can just dern sure hold your business till the next crop comes in." This time we all howled with laughter and it continued off and on throughout the entire meal. Jess, without knowing it, became the unspoken hero that day. I was no longer embarrassed and most of all, I could tell that sunshine had finally returned to Mama's soul.

After that day, Mama and Daddy would often stay up way after they had settled Jess and me into bed, talking and making plans. From time to time, one of us would wake up pretending to want water or just to be held for a little while. Mama would then tend to our needs and because of it being so cold, she would warm our blanket in front of the fire and then tuck us back in bed. One morning after the long winter had finally broken, Mama and Daddy shared with us what they had been talking about now for the last several weeks. We were going to be moving to Daddy Jack's place. It was where my mother had grown up and lived until she and Daddy had met and married. "A place full of heart treasures," she'd say. Even though I hated leaving all my friends in town, I would come to find many a treasure myself on that old plantation.

Chapter 2

Off to the Plantation

The house we moved into was a sturdy wooden structure that had been built with rough lumber and logs, all cut from the plantation that surrounded it. Many times we had heard the story of how the land had been settled in the early 1800's by my mother's great grandpa Silas and his wife Minnie.

Grandpa Silas had followed General Jackson, fighting against the Creek Indians and while doing so, had gotten a bird's-eye view of the rich and fertile land that sat next to the Pea River. After the war, he gathered his wife and belongings in South Carolina and came back to homestead here. They say that over time, Silas acquired more land and brought in slaves to clear and work the place, eventually naming it Melrose Plantation. Even though we had visited and stayed many times over the years, Melrose now belonged to us, and there were lots of new adventures Jess and I would have between what we called Wampus Cat Creek, which marked one side of our land, to just past the swampy woods where the Pea River flowed. There was one area which looked dark and spooky to us, and we avoided it. We had been told that there was an old Indian burial ground in that patch of woods. Ghosts and strange noises had been seen and heard in there, and if we ever did have to pass by the place, it was in a trot.

Not far from our house and just down from what we called the cherry-tree field was where Ol' Doolah lived. He and his parents, as well as many others who had long since passed away, had been the slaves on this plantation. They had worked the land together, row after row and season after season, and were considered to be more like family members than anything else. Everything that was made, hunted, or harvested was shared by all, and God, as it was noted by Ol' Doolah, blessed the land and everyone on it.

There was seldom a week that went by that Jess or I failed to take some Indian treasures we had found to Ol' Doolah's door – arrowheads, pieces of a clay pipe or pottery we had uncovered in a field or down by the creek. Doolah would study each and every find with his old and yellowed eyes, comment how this small arrowhead must have been used to hunt birds or squirrels, while the larger ones were for hunting deer or maybe even bear. The pottery, he said, was made from clay probably found down by the river and would have been set right in the middle of a fire to cook some type of stew. The pipes were used by the men, who would fill them with rabbit tobacco for a smoke. "It still grows wild over this whole land," he said, waving his hand from side to side. "Can you show us some?" both Jess and I asked, jumping to our feet. "Why, sho' I can. I seen some just behind the hen house this mawnin," he said reaching out for me and Jess to help him up. Right where he said it would be, we harvested eight or ten of the grayish plants. We thanked him and after gathering up our goods, we told him we'd best be getting home.

Once we got there, we proudly showed off our finds, including the rabbit tobacco, to Mama and Daddy. Daddy then told us how when he was a young boy, he and some friends would gather the same type of tobacco by the sack full and sell it to folks who had come into town to stock up on goods. "That was when the supply of regular tobacco couldn't be counted on," he said. "You'll need to hang it above the fireplace there and let it dry awhile before it'd be fit for the pipe, you know," said Daddy, motioning to some nails that stuck out from the mantle. "I'm sure we can find some reed sticks here 'bouts that would put your pipe in working order," Daddy assured, "and after we come back from church and the mill tomorrow evenin, your weed oughta be ready to smoke," he said with a grin.

Daddy had been partners with Mr. Wiley Poach for over twenty years. Together they owned and ran the only cotton ginning company in Enterprise. Since cotton was a seasonal crop, the gin would operate only several months out of the year. The workers they employed didn't mind, with many of them giving up harder jobs for awhile, so they could draw a fair wage and stay in from the weather for a bit. Jess and I liked most of the men who worked at the gin. For with all the foolishness they carried on, there never seemed to be a dull moment or conversation. Though operations were not set to begin for several more months, Daddy wanted Mr. Hiram, the foreman, and Benny, who was very strong and handy for lifting purposes, to meet him before church to inspect some of the machinery before the season started. Mr. Hiram, prompt as usual, showed up at 9:00 a.m. After greeting us all, he inquired whether we had been bothered by last night's storm. Then as we were talking, Benny came limping up, all covered in mud and favoring his right leg. "If you want to hurt your leg real good just bang it against those hitches out there," Benny said, still rubbing his shin.

"Now why in the hog snot would I want to do that for?" Mr. Hiram asked, looking as if the dumbest person he ever met had just made an entrance into his life. We all knew Benny was a little on the slow side. He was prone to some very unusual habits, such as swatting at things that weren't really there and at times hollering out for no good reason. His mother ran a boarding house just down the street from our gin and was grateful to have him away from the guests as often as possible. Occasionally, she would even have folks come through and stay who were from abroad. This, she thought, elevated her social standing in the community and made her a little more cultured than others. It was after one such guest had visited that Benny began speaking with a British accent.

"I know he ain't right in the head," Mr. Hiram said, after hearing him talk like that for about a week, "but by gosh if he calls me ol' chap one more time, I swear he'll leave this place a eunuch!"

Of course, all the other workers knew how aggravating Benny was to Mr. Hiram and would add to the situation by having Benny ask all types of unnecessary questions right before the gin was started each morning. One year, they even put Benny up to borrowing the company's mule and wagon so he could follow the fireman's band through town on its way to the annual Independence Day festival. After the wagon had been decorated and the mule hitched up, one of the men got an eight-foot piece of rope and strung a dead goat to one of the back wheels, making it look as if Benny had forgotten to untie him before he'd gotten under way. Benny, not knowing any different, started up the wagon and proceeded down Main Street right behind the band. All along the route, people hollered and were trying to bring his attention to the fact that he had dragged the poor goat to its death. Not understanding them because of the band and other noises, Benny just smiled and waved, even taking the time to bow for the mayor on his way by. From that day on folks would say "Here comes *B-e-n-n-y*" when they'd see him coming, stretching his name out just like it was being nannied by a goat.

After everything was found to be in order at the gin, we loaded up in the carriage and headed to church. It was Pastor Seth's custom to greet everyone as they entered the church house, and since it had been a spell since we'd last been there, he inspected both Jess and me with a close eye. "My goodness, how you two have grown since I last saw you! What have they been feedin y'all at Melrose?" he asked, smiling. "Just cat guts and collards," Jess answered without hesitating, for he had heard Daddy say this many a time in jest to Mama when asked what special dishes he wanted cooked. "Well, I'm sure your mama does a fine job, whatever she cooks up," Pastor Seth said laughing and probably recalling that Jess would say and do just about anything.

Now most of the time I never paid church nor Preacher Seth's sermons any attention. Both Jess and I would sleep through the services once we got the singing part out of the way. But this particular Sunday I seemed to hang onto every word Pastor Seth said. I think it was the story he started with that caught my attention.

"There once was a farmer who, on a very cold and windy night, left the warmth of his fire so his animals could be fed and seen about. On his way to the barn, he heard the whistling of some little finches who had perched themselves in a nearby tree, trying desperately to keep themselves warm. The farmer, knowing the birds would be much warmer inside the barn, opened both doors and hung his lantern inside to draw attention. Then the farmer circled around behind the tree trying to shoo the little birds into the barn. Several times, the farmer tried shooing the birds, but they only fled in different directions. He tried whistling for them at the entrance of the barn, but they wouldn't come. He even tried making a trail of bread crumbs, but the little birds would have no part of his coaxing. Finally realizing that to them he must seem like some kind of large and fierce creature, he stood still, wishing that just for a moment he could become one of them so they would know he meant them no harm and that his intentions were only good. It was also at that moment that it became clear to the farmer what God had done for him when he became a man and had come to live here on this earth."

What Pastor Seth said and how he said it made perfect sense to my little mind, and even though he preached on for quite some time, it was that story that had set up in me. After awhile, he finally asked everyone to bow their heads for prayer and for those who wanted to pray and ask this same God who had come all those years ago to come and live in our hearts. So it was on that day in the tenth year of my life that I asked God to do that. Then after we were dismissed and about to leave the church grounds, I hurried back inside, finding Pastor Seth right inside the door stacking hymnals. "Pastor," I said, "I wanted you to know that was the finest sermon I ever stayed awake for and tell you I asked God to come and live in my heart today." I then turned on my heel and sprinted for our buggy.

It was unlike Daddy's partner Mr. Wiley or his wife Miss Daffy to be absent from any church service, and since he and Miss Daffy were to be leaving for Mobile the next day, in regards to his and daddy's ginning business, Daddy thought it'd be a good idea to check on them. Once we got there, we noticed Doc Matthews's carriage pulled up in the yard. "You and Jess stay in the buggy," Daddy said, as he and Mama climbed out and walked with a quick step up onto the porch.

"Do ya think somebody's died in there?" Jess asked me after we had sat for a few minutes.

"Naw, if somebody had a died, there'd be buzzards circlin' around up yonder," I said, pointing above the house.

Finally, the doctor and Miss Daffy came out to the front porch. "He'll need to stay off that foot for at least a week," Doc said. "I'll check back in on him in a few days and if he's behaved, I'll leave him some crutches."

After Doc cleared the porch, Miss Daffy smiled and motioned for Jess and me to come on inside. "What happened to Mr. Wiley?" I asked kinda quiet-like, not knowing whether he was asleep, for it seemed like doctors were always wanting their patients to get some sleep.

"He'll be fine, chillun. Mr. Wiley just got his foot caught crossways in a hole somehow, tryin to catch a fryer this mornin; twisted his ankle right bad, too. Bet he'll specially enjoy eatin this one!" she said, laughing heartily. "But I'm sure seeing you two is just the medicine he needs right now."

Mr. Wiley doted on me and Jess. He always acted excited to see us and kept peppermint sticks handy for the times when we might be around. He and Miss Daffy had no children left of their own, having lost both of their boys to the yellow fever years before.

"I'm sure you, Anna and the kids will love a few days in Mobile." Mr Wiley said, while kicking at his bed covers. "Last I saw that place was when I mustered into the army way back in '62. I was only 16 then. Couldn't wait to leave those hot fields I worked in everyday. If I had only known what that was gonna be like. My god, Winford! There were times towards the end of that war I was so hungry I'd a give a month's pay to just crawl up and eat the slop we use to feed our hogs back home. It was a fool's errand we was on!" he shouted, startling everyone within ear shot. Then catching himself, said, "I'm sorry, Winford, but ever now and then the memories are still fresh. And lyin here in the middle of the day don't help none," he said, still trying to get comfortable. "You go and take the family with ya. It's just a one-day trip by train and I'm sure they'd all enjoy getting to see the sights. Really grown a lot from what I've read in the papers, ships and cargo comin in from all over the world." Then glancing around the room he saw mine and Jess's excited looks. "Well, now—where did these two good lookin young'uns come from?" he said, waving us closer.

Chapter 3

The Big City

With the whistle blowing, our train pulled out of the station at ten o'clock that next morning. Jess and I ran from one side of the car to the other waving out the windows at anybody who would pay attention to us. Daddy sat reading the newspaper like our adventure was old hat to him,while Mama made a list of things she'd like to shop for once we got to Mobile. After we had been gone for no less than an hour or so, the bottom seemed to just drop out of the sky. When it rained at home, both Daddy and I would pull a chair up to the nearest window and watch it for as long as it would last. It had been a good while since I had cuddled up to my daddy, but once he put his paper down, I became his little girl again and crawled up beside him. There we sat, quietly watching it rain until I couldn't stay awake any longer.

I must have slept through several stops before we finally changed trains around Pensacola, and unlike the previous car, we were now almost packed. "What's all them bullet holes fer in the panels?" one man asked as the conductor came down the aisle checking tickets.

"Way I heard it, we had us a real bad man on this train bout 20 year ago," the conductor said. "Was one of them gunfightin fellers outta Texas, name a John Wesley Hardin. He was hidin out with his wife and kids over in Pollard and goin by the last name a Swain. Anyway, ol' John Hardin had a hankern to go over into Mobile ever so often to do some gambling. The rangers outta Texas caught wind of his habits somehow, sat right here on this here train car as he was headed back to Pollard one night. They let him get good and relaxed before they pulled their iron on him. Some of his friends was kilt in the scrape, but Hardin was spared 'cause he got his gun caught up in his 'spenders and was clubbed over the head. Heard they hauled him back to Texas for his trial and he's still serving time outchonder in one of them prisons."

Of course, Jess and I were spellbound by the conductor's tale and knew we could now pretty much one-up anybody's story with this one, if we ever needed to.

The hustle and bustle of Mobile was unlike anything I had ever seen. We were greeted with a number of men hollering the moment we stepped from the train. "Take your bags, Sir?" one man yelled while another hoisted the bags up onto his carriage.

"Yes, that will be fine, and we need a good hotel or boarding house," Daddy said while taking his wallet out of his breast pocket. The man nodded and once we were all secure, he took off as if he had been invited to his last meal. The streets we traveled on were all paved with brick, and most of them were lighted on each side by tall black posts. Shouting and laughter could be heard from all directions and more than once, I heard gun shots fired—but at whom or what I could not tell. I was much happier once we reached our place of lodging and was hoping that by morning, things would be much calmer outside.

"Y'all made it just in time for supper," the lady said as if she were expecting us. "I'm Kate Shepard, but most folks just call me Kitty." Then without waiting for a return of greetings, she hollered for Roy, who was already standing behind her. "Take these bags upstairs to the Bay Room, and while you're up there, please make sure everything is in order for these folks." Then, looking at me and Jess, she whispered, "If you eat all your supper, I'll treat you to a story about hidden pirate treasure and a peg-legged ghost. Now, go wash up!"

We joined several other folks already seated around a large table that had a turn-and-grab in the middle. "Just help yourselves and if there's anything you need, just holler for Roy and he'll fetch it," Miss Kitty said. Then holding her nose and a plate full of food, she stepped out onto the back porch where a young boy sat all by himself.

"He got sprayed by a pole cat the other day," said one of the men who was sitting at the table. "Can't even get the dogs to play with him. Wish I could borrow him to hang around my mother-in-law for awhile," he said, as everyone busted out laughing. I felt true pity for the boy as he sat there swatting flies and trying to make the best of a fine meal. Then without warning and probably because of the laughter he had heard, he showed up at our table asking for a piece of bread.

"Yes, by God! Here, take two!" the same man said while covering his nose with a napkin.

"Thank you, sir, and I hope your stay here is a pleasant one," the boy said, patting the man on his shoulder. And then with a huge grin, the boy slowly went back to his solitude.

With everyone finished with dinner, we all moved out onto the front porch, hoping to catch a breeze off the bay. As we sat enjoying the evening, another carriage pulled up and out stepped a man and his wife and their two children about the same ages as Jess and me. "Well, we finally made it," the man yelled to Miss Kitty, who had gone down on the sidewalk to see what their business was.

"Made it for what?" she asked.

The man replied, "We are the Harold Mims family. I telegraphed you over a week ago telling you what day me and my family would be arriving. My uncle told me to request the Bay Room from you because of the scenery. Don't you remember the wire I sent? You replied that all would be in order for us when we arrived, and you would even have your buggy waiting at the station."

"Oh, my Lord!" Miss Kitty exclaimed, grabbing her head. "You mean you're not those people up there on the porch?" she asked while pointing up to us.

"Apparently not," the man replied, beginning to get aggravated.

"My Lord a mighty, I rented out your room an hour ago to those folks!" said Miss Kitty, again pointing in our direction. With this, the man gave a glaring look at us and then with a few choice words stomped back to his carriage.

"Bet that man don't preach for a livin!" one guest remarked as Miss Kitty climbed the steps, blushing with embarrassment at her mistake.

"No, and I will not have anyone stayin here what cain't hold his temper and what shows bad manners in front of children," she said, trying to conceal her chagrin.

"There are special places for those kinda folks," said another guest.

"Yeah, and they are all up north," the first replied back as Miss Kitty walked inside fanning herself. Needless to say, Jess and me never got our story.

The next day Mama took us shopping while Daddy went to his appointment. He was supposed to meet with two men from England who were stationed in Mobile for the purpose of buying ginned cotton for their clothing mills. Mr. Wiley had read an advertisement that their company would pay top dollar for premium ginned cotton and had made arrangements by wire for Daddy to meet with them. Knowing his meeting would last for awhile, Daddy gave Mama fifteen dollars for her quests and warned her not to be taken advantage of by any gypsies.

The shops were only a short walk from Miss Kitty's house and once we reached them, Mama went right to work sizing me and Jess for all sorts of clothes. "Hold this up in front of you," she told me and Jess no less than a dozen times. Then finally after she had satisfied our needs, she began to pick out a few items for herself. "Good Lord, I can't wear that; my legs would show!" Mama said, placing a dress back on the rack. Mama was one to say her thoughts out loud. "What does he expect me to buy with fifteen dollars? Watch out for gypsies! I'll show him gypsy," she said, holding something up in front of a mirror. After Mama quit talking to herself, she made arrangements with the store manager for our packages to be delivered to Miss Kitty's. Then we continued to look into every store window up and down Government Street.

Mobile was by far the biggest city I had ever been to. We had read a little about it in school, and our teacher Mrs. Newt had told us all about the annual celebration they had down here called Mardi Gras. "You haven't seen the elephant till you've seen that festival," she'd say in a know-it-all voice. Being a kid, I really didn't understand why grown folks made a fuss over such things. I was happy just finding a crawdad in the creek or making an owl hoot back at me. Fancy stuff didn't matter at my age, and I was sure if we had to endure another minute of looking at doodads in window displays, it would be the death of me. Then when all hope seemed to be lost and I was expecting the buzzards to start circling, we stumbled upon what must have been a gift sent straight from Heaven: Miss Maci's Ice Cream Parlor. After leaving the parlor, I realized my Big Thank You List to God was now up to three. Black Jack Chewing Gum, seeing that General Bob was still alive after his fall, and now, caramel fudge ice cream.

By the time we got back to Miss Kitty's, Daddy had finished his appointment and was waiting on the porch for us. "Well, I got some real good news" he announced. "The fellas I met with said my samples was some of the finest cotton they had ever seen. Said they'd pay top dollar for everything we could send 'em! Good Lord willin and the Creek Injuns don't rise, looks like we'll be a doin business with them folks for some time to come." Then without a warning, Daddy jumped up from his chair and started dancing and woo-hooing like an Indian. Jess and I plumb laughed till we couldn't see straight while Mama stood there shaking her head and wondering whether the state insane asylum might be short one person.

Chapter 4

The Outlaws

The trip back home to Enterprise seemed to take twice as long. It didn't help any that Mama kept quizzing me and Jess from school books that Miss Kitty had given her the day before we left Mobile. When Miss Kitty had settled down long enough, she had given us all a room-by-room tour of her home. The room she was the most excited about had ten desks and a chalk board with all the letters already written on it. She had a great big globe sitting up on a pedestal by her desk and three stacks of books that were almost as tall as me. She called this her Dream Room. "Children need a good education, you know," she said, looking down at Jess and me. "I may not be able to reach all the children in this city, but by crackie, I intend to bless the ones God sends my way," she said while pounding emphatically on her desk.

With our lessons learned, we finally pulled into the Enterprise depot only to find the streets near 'bout empty. "Some kinda plague goin round?" Daddy asked one station man.

"Naw sir, most the folks is out to the cemetery at Mr. Ketchum's funeral," he said pointing over his shoulder. "Bank got robbed day fore yesterday. The buncha low life sheep dung prob'ly beat Mr. Ketchum to death after he was good enough to open the safe for 'em. Nobody found him till the next mornin. Sheriff and a posse been out huntin their tracks ever since, but I think it's mostly useless now 'cause a the storm last night."

"My Lord," Daddy said, his voice quivering. "That man was one of the finest people I've ever known. There won't be a drop of pity for those men once they're pulled from whatever hole they're a hidin in. They have no idea what a fine man and citizen they've taken from us!" Then after Daddy tipped the man to unload and watch our bags, we all walked to the cemetery to pay our respects.

Our ride home was somber. Whenever Daddy was upset about something, he rarely spoke a word. About halfway there we ran into Sheriff Tyril and a posse of men. "Guess y'all heard bout Mr. Ketchum," the sheriff said as we pulled to the side of the road.

"Yep," Daddy said with a slow nod. "Any ideas at all where they might be holed up?" he asked the sheriff.

"It's anybody's guess now. We lost their tracks bout ten miles back. Storm kept spookin our horses and washed all their sign away to boot. Gonna wire Ketchum's friend the Governor when I get back to town and see what kinda reward he might put out. If it's big enough, I figure somebody'll flush 'em out for us. Keep your eyes open, folks," the sheriff warned sternly. "Desperate men will do anything!"

After we got home, Daddy set about cleaning and checking every gun we had. "I don't think we'll have any trouble," he said. "Most folks on the run tend to get as far away as possible once they've done their deed. Never hurts to be ready, though." Then sensing that Jess and me might be scared from it all, he changed the subject. "Looks like your tobacky is dry now," he said, pointing across the room toward our harvest of rabbit tobacco. "If you want, I can rig up the pipe y'all found, and we'll all have us a smoke." I had watched Daddy smoke his pipe for years now, and it seemed like it was something he used as a reward for all the hard working or thinking he did. Both Jess and I would ask him from time to time if we could have a puff, but he would always just smile and say it was for grown folks and not kids.

"Grown folks get all the good things in life," Jess would say, stomping his foot.

"Well, if you really want to smoke that bad, find ya some rabbit tobacky," Daddy would say. Now finally, after all these times of wanting and waiting, I was beginning to think this may be another thing I could add to my list of Big Thank Yous to God.

"I wanna be first," Jess said, jumping up and down. "I never get to be first for nothin!"

"All right then, just give me a minute," Daddy said. Then after hunting about in the yard for awhile, Daddy came back in with a little reed stick that he'd trimmed down so it would fit nice and tight into the clay pipe we had found.

While Daddy loaded the pipe, Jess stood by making faces at me. It really didn't matter, knowing I'd be next, but just for good measure I stuck my tongue out to make him think he'd got one up on me. Then after Daddy had packed in the rabbit tobacco, he handed Jess the pipe and told him what to do once he put the fire to it.

"I already know bout that," Jess said, as if he'd smoked before.

"Then go to it, boy," Daddy answered, putting his match to the pipe. Once it had gotten lit proper, Jess stepped back and took a big draw while cradling the other end with several fingers and looking just as cocky as if he'd brought in a big crop of cotton. Then all of a sudden, Jess's face had a look and a color I'd never seen before. He slung the pipe down hard, busting it all to pieces, and began running around the room in circles while fanning his mouth and tongue, which was now hanging out of his mouth, red as a fox's tail. He kept trying to scream or holler for us to get him something, but by now Daddy was laughing so hard he couldn't stand up and Mama, who knew Daddy was teaching us a lesson this whole time, ran for the outhouse for fear she'd wet herself. Finally, after Jess had made about five laps, he broke for the kitchen and grabbed a cup of water that had been set out for us before we started our smoke. After Jess drank and spit for what seemed like half an hour, he came back into the room looking at Daddy with a scowl on his face.

Daddy, who by now had stopped laughing, busted out again and hollered at Jess, "Well, how bout a shot a whiskey then?!" Needless to say after seeing what happened to Jess, I decided to pass on ever taking my turn with the pipe.

For several days after learning about Mr. Ketchum, Daddy slept with a shotgun next to the bed and also carried a pistol whenever he went outside. He made Jess and me stay close to the house, and more than once we saw him checking on us whenever we went to the privy or played in the yard.

It wasn't until Pastor Seth came out to visit one day that Daddy seemed to finally relax a little. "I brought you the newspaper, Winford," the preacher said. "They got a $1,000 reward for any information leadin to those men's arrest and conviction," he said, shaking the paper a bit. "Most the folks in town think it's a long shot they'll ever get caught. No description of the men and from what the sheriff thinks, they prob'ly split up and went separate ways as well," he said as Daddy nodded in agreement. "Let me state the real reason I'm here, Winford" the preacher said while reaching into his pocket. "I got a letter the other day from a friend of mine in Huntsville, a fellow pastor whom I've known for over twenty years. Besides his own congregational duties, he's also been ministerin to six families who were sharecroppin in that area. The land they been workin on has played out, and they've been asked to vacate the property. I remembered the last time we spoke, you had mentioned the possibility of sharecroppin some a the land out here. 'Course if you did want these folks, you'd have to pay their fare."

Daddy sat there for a little while and then with tears beginning to fill his eyes, he said, "Preacher, the last several days I've mostly been thinkin about Mr. Ketchum. He was a good man to me and anyone who ever came to him for help. He loaned me money to buy into the gin when nobody else would even consider it. He never looked down on anybody but would be the first one to reach down and help others up. The other day when I was chorin around outside I told the Lord if he'd let me live another good spell I'd try my best to be like that man. You tell your friend to let them know we'll be waitin on 'em, and they can stay at the mill 'til we can make arrangements out here," Daddy said, wiping his face. "I'll send word to the station, and I'll cover their tickets even if I have to borrow the money."

"Praise the good Lord and know that you won't be the only one carryin this load, Winford," the preacher said all excited-like. "We've already had members of our church come forward with pledges of food and supplies if it worked out for these folks to find employment down here."

Then after we had all saw him to his buggy, the preacher turned and looked at me. "Janie, every now and then, I do preach a good sermon," he said with a big smile. "Won't be too long 'til the water around here'll be good and warmed up; need to see bout gettin you baptized."

After the preacher had left, Daddy motioned for us to follow him out to the barn. "I'm gonna see what shape those rail cars are in," Daddy said, gathering up some tools. "'Speck they'll need some work to make for a proper livin place, but at least it'll keep 'em off the ground." Daddy was referring to some old rail cars that had been used by the Confederacy to transport troops. Once the cause was falling apart, the government ordered the cars to be detached from the engine and left sitting on some side tracks so it could move faster and not be captured by the Yankees. Several years later, a company came through and took up all the rails except for the little portion these cars had been sitting on. Knowing they were abandoned now, Daddy Jack patched them up and used the cars to store his cotton and hay in. I had only been in them once a few years back when we had been out riding around the place and were caught up in a hail storm. We all went up into the cars, which were mostly empty then.

I remember Daddy Jack pointing at the walls where soldiers had once carved their names and regiment numbers. "Ya know, I lost both my brothers in that war," he said real solemn-like. "They left home thinkin they'd be back in a month or two at the most. Now Leonard's buried high up on some mountain in Chattanooga, and Russell, well we heard he was kilt by cannon fire fightin under General Joe Johnston. His regiment commander wrote us sayin they buried him where he fell right next to a little crick where he was getting water for everybody. That was outside of Atlanta in '64."

After we had loaded the tools and some rough lumber into the wagon, we headed out toward the rail cars, which sat about a quarter mile from where Ol' Doolah lived. Just a few yards from his house, he came out waving us down. "Mr. Winford, somebody done stole 'bout half my layin hens last night. Wadn't no fox or bobcat, neither. I saw shoe tracks," Doolah said.

"Could you tell how many folks were in on it?" Daddy asked.

"Naw suh, them tracks wuz one on top of another," Doolah said shaking his head.

Knowing how large our plantation was, Daddy realized it'd be a mighty troublesome trip to make for just a few hens. "I think whoever did it ain't that far away," Daddy said, "unless they like their chicken raw. You still got that ol' scatter gun Daddy Jack gave you?" he asked.

"Yes, Suh," Doolah nodded.

"Good. Then hang tight to it. If anybody comes snoopin around, don't think twiced bout givin 'em both barrels," he said. "I'm gonna turn back for the house right now, but I'll be here in the mornin to check on you. If you ain't out and about yet I'll whistle for ya." Though he never said it out loud, we could tell what Daddy was thinkin. Three outlaws were still on the loose and probably close by. If they were the ones who had done this and he could get word to the sheriff, there might be a chance to catch them before they moved on. Once we got back home, Daddy went inside and wasted no time in making his guns handy again. "I'm gonna set down to the main road for awhile and see if I can't catch someone headed into town," Daddy said. "If I'm lucky, the sheriff and some men could be out here in the mornin so I won't have to go this alone."

"You just don't be a fool about this, Winford," Mama said. "If it's the same men, you'll need all the help you can get. The last thing we need is to be singin some sad song over your grave!"

Daddy kinda frowned at the thought of what Mama said, but didn't give an argument. "I'll be back directly," he said, snapping the reins. About two hours later, we heard him outside pulling the wagon to a stop. "Caught ol' Beanard Puckett headed toward town with a load a mail," Daddy said. "He's gonna carry the message in for me post haste. Hopefully, the sheriff and some men'll make it here by first light, and we can get this thing over with. Now if you ain't got no objections 'bout that, let's eat 'fore I starve to death and y'all have to start singin them songs."

I was much older before I learned all the bits and pieces of what happened that next day. Some came from the sheriff himself. Others I read from newspaper accounts mama had saved over the years, and then of course, I was there when it all started at daybreak that morning.

"Winford, I hope your hunch is right about these men," the sheriff said. "You got ideas where they might be right now?" he asked.

"There's only one place I'd put 'em at, Sheriff, and that's the ol' rail cars," Daddy said. "There's water not far behind 'em with the creek, and anybody would prefer to sleep off the ground and outa the weather if'n they had the chance. Last time I was out there, it had grown up a lot all around them, so it'd make for some good cover."

"We'll follow you out there and you can show us the best way to approach the cars. Maybe we can catch 'em still sleepin if we're lucky," Sheriff Tyril said.

Then Daddy and the men trotted off armed to the teeth, hoping to find Mr. Ketchum's murderers. "I'm gonna whistle for Ol' Doolah," Daddy announced, approaching Doolah's house and giving a bird whistle.

After a few seconds, Doolah stepped outside. "I smelt smoke last night, Mr. Winford; it was comin about midnight from over dat way." Doolah pointed in the direction of the rail cars.

"Let's tie our horses up here," Daddy said. "Then we can walk up closer and figure which car they're in." After tying their horses off on Doolah's porch posts, the sheriff's posse walked through a little patch of trees and then another hundred yards until they could see the rail cars. "There's seven cars and only one of 'em has doors on both sides. It's the one on the far end. That'd be my guess," Daddy whispered.

After looking down both sides and not seeing any horses, the sheriff directed one of the men to the creek. "Ease down there and see if you can't spot their horses."

While his deputy was gone, Daddy saw a whiff of smoke rise up from in front of the last rail car. "They're down there, Sheriff," Daddy said, pointing. "See the smoke?"

"Let's wait for my man to get back and we'll split up on each side and smoke 'em out," the sheriff replied.

In a few minutes, the deputy came back and held up two fingers. "I could see where another one went off by the creek not too long ago," he said.

"Don't that crick wind around behind Doolah's house?" the sheriff asked.

"It does," Daddy said. "It twists its way over behind our house, too, if'n you go far enough," Daddy added, worried-like.

"I'm gonna grab me an arm full of this dead grass and throw it on their fire. If we're lucky it'll smoke 'em out the back door without much of a fight," the sheriff said. "One a you men cover me with a rifle and the other three go around to the other side. When they come out, fire once in the air and then holler for 'em to lay down."

The sheriff pulled up the grass and eased along one rail car after another till he got close by the last one. "If anybody sticks his head out while I'm puttin this on the fire, you shoot 'im," the sheriff said in a whisper. Then, knowing he was covered, he eased down and crawled over to the smoldering fire, putting the grass on top of it.

Then just as quietly, he crawled backwards to where his deputy was. "Let's give it a minute and see what happens," he said, motioning for them to both get in a better spot. The grass finally caught fire and smoke started drifting through the front door of the car.

Another minute or two, and the men could be heard talking from inside. "I thought you put that fire out last night," one of the men said real mean-like to another.

"Naw, I didn't have no water and I dern shore wadn't gonna pour whiskey on it," the other said. "Sides, it was just a little flicker once we went to bed down!"

"You're an idiot," the first man said as he peeped out a crack towards the fire. "If'n I had my way we wouldn't split nothin with you. Not even them chickens we caught."

Turns out the smoke had done little but wake the men up and the sheriff knew it. "You men inside there," the sheriff hollered, "this is the law and we got both your doors covered. You come out right now or we set the car on fire." After several seconds and no reply, the sheriff began firing into the walls of the car, but not a single shot was returned.

"What are they thinkin'?" the sheriff said mostly to himself.

Then after another minute or two he heard one of his deputies from the other side hollering, "They're goin for our horses, Sheriff!" The two men had dropped down through a hole in the floor of the rail car. Being concealed by the high grass, they crawled under all six of the other cars until they made it out to the end where they broke and ran for the trees the posse had come through.

"My god, we've lost 'em for sure now," the sheriff said. "And they're gonna get away on our mounts!" Then pointing toward the creek, he ordered one of the deputies to get the outlaws' horses. "We ain't got much time!" he hollered. Then just as the deputy sprinted off, they heard shooting on the other side of the woods close to Ol' Doolah's house.

"He gave 'em both barrels by gosh," Daddy said, starting to run that way with the others behind him. By the time they reached Doolah's house, one man was lying in the road and Doolah was slumped back against his house. The sheriff and his deputies ran up to the outlaw while Daddy made it over to Doolah.

"I got 'em both, Mr. Winford. The other one, that plugged me, I speck he won't make it but a piece or more for he be down, too," Doolah said, spitting up blood.

"You did fine, Doolah, just fine," Daddy said, knowing that Doolah had been shot in the lung and was done for. "You just rest easy now; we'll see bout getting you fixed up." Then grabbing Daddy's hand, Doolah whispered these last sweet words from his lips: "You tells Jess......and Miss Janie.........I says..........to come sees me."

"Winford!" the sheriff hollered. "We got this man to talk fore he died. He said the one that was gone when we got here this mornin would be over around Haw Ridge gettin food and such. We got a description of him and what he's mounted on. The other man my deputy found down the road a piece, wadn't nothin we could do for him. One a my deputies will stay out here with you and borrow your wagon to take these bodies to town. Check out that rail car for money and bank notes, if you will." He said, spurring his horse.

Daddy and the deputy laid Ol' Doolah out on the porch and began wrapping him up with a bed sheet. Before covering his face, Daddy stroked it several times while tears rolled down his own. The deputy stepped back and took his hat off in respect.

"God never made a more gentle soul in this world," Daddy said. "My children will carry him in their minds and hearts forever. I 'spect I will, too." Then, after covering Doolah's face, they walked outside to finish the business Sheriff Tyril had requested.

Chapter 5

Sharecroppers

According to the papers, the third outlaw the sheriff and his deputies had gone after already had several warrants for his arrest. Wanted for two previous murders in Mississippi and federal offenses against the postal service, he sat in the Coffee County jail for over two weeks cussing anyone within ear shot and bragging about his exploits. After the man tried to escape and bashed the head of a deputy in the process, Judge Sweat, who was over the district court at that time, called for a trial to quell the sentiment of the local citizens, knowing that soon they would take matters into their own hands. The prisoner Thomas A. Burrows was found guilty and hung two days later behind Dickens Feed and Lumber. Of course, Daddy would not allow me and Jess to attend such an event, but we were with him at the courthouse several days later when Judge Sweat asked Daddy to step into his office.

"Winford, I'm catchin flak from the state attorney in Mississippi for havin that prisoner hung before he could stand trial for his crimes over there. I thought I'd read you my reply before I posted it."

"Oh, go ahead," Daddy said, knowing the judge was one not to be syrupy with his words.

Dear Sir:

I have received your letter and it is true I have saved your state a great deal of money in the transport and legal funds the prisoner would have incurred your tax payers and for that, Sir, you are most welcome. The prisoner you are referring to admitted to the crimes he committed in our fine county, including an escape attempt and assaulting a deputy during the process. I saw no reason to contact you before or during our legal processes; however, I have spoken to our local mortician, and he has agreed to dig the stiff-legged son of a snake up if you wish for us to transport him to your state for re-hanging. Please wire sufficient monies, and we would be glad to freight his body to you on the next train out. I am sure you will find the aforementioned to be much more co-operative than we did. Please let me know if these are your wishes.

> *Signed,*
> *District Judge J. A. Sweat*
> *Coffee County, Alabama*

As far as the money that was taken from the bank, it was in a saddle bag found dropped under one of the rail cars by the fleeing outlaws. The few dollars that were missing had purchased whiskey and supplies, all of which Burrows was carrying when Sheriff Tyril apprehended him. Once all the necessary reports were filed and signed off on, the sheriff showed up at our house several weeks later with a reward check for $1,000 and a proclamation from the governor's office, which was also printed in the town's newspaper later that week. It read:

From the Governor's Office, State of Alabama, April 14th, 1906:

Let it be known by all men that on March 15th, 1906, Dison Winford Taylor of Coffee County, Alabama, did act in a brave and courageous manner.

His quick and responsive acts of contacting necessary authorities and further participation in the pursuit and ensuing gun battle against wanted fugitives has brought about a swift and just conclusion to the participants in a most heinous crime. Let it be further noted that this proclamation has been read and recognized on the floor of the Alabama State Legislature as to the above said actions taken by Dison Winford Taylor, a loyal and noted citizen of our great state.

Signed and sealed by my hand April 14th, 1906:

William Dorsey Jelks, Governor, State of Alabama

"Sheriff Tyril, that reward was the furtherest thing from my mind and the last thing I ever expected when I saw you ridin up," Daddy said.

"That ain't all, Winford. The bank itself has taken out a $200 dollar credit for you at Hemp Smith's store. Said you could use it whenever you want. They're just grateful their customer's money was returned. Most of which was Hemp Smith's anyway," the sheriff said laughing. Daddy just stood there completely speechless. "You deserve every penny, Winford," the sheriff said. "Your hunch about their whereabouts was right on the nose. By the way, Pastor Seth wanted me to tell you the sharecroppers' train is due in tomorrow bout noon time." Then tipping his hat to me and Mama, he bid us farewell.

Still in shock, Daddy handed the check and governor's letter to Mama. "Anna, is this whole thing a dream or did it really happen?"

"Yes, Winford, it all happened. Some people would even say you're a hero," Mama said with a smile.

"A hero!" Daddy exclaimed. "Huh! I'm about as much a hero as some ol' bug around here would be."

"Well, I'll keep this money for myself then," Mama said laughing. "And I'll be sure to watch out for gypsies, too!"

The next morning, we all loaded up and went to town to deposit Daddy's check and meet with the families who would be arriving. Pastor Seth had already sent word that he and several members from the church would be at the gin setting up food for everyone, and Mr. Wiley had come to the station to welcome the families, too. "Well, Winford, I know you must be plumb wore out from all the excitement that happened out at your place, but I'm just glad you and yours are all safe and well," he said, winkin at Jess and me.

"Yes, sir, I'm glad it's all over with, too. I wouldn't wish that kinda thing on nobody," Daddy said. "By the way, I think we can gather up enough loose cotton from around the gin to make some soft beds for the folks 'til you're ready for them at Melrose," Mr. Wiley suggested.

"That's a good idea. I hope it won't take more than a few days to get those old rail cars fixed up. I figure any money I have to put out on these folks to make them feel at home should be a privilege on my behalf," Daddy said. "Especially since God has seen fit to bless me in the midst of other folks' tragedies."

Late as usual, the train finally pulled into the station and began unloading. "Lookin for a Mr. Taylor," one man said, sort of leading the others.

"Mr. Taylor was my father and he died twelve years ago. So if you'll just call me Winford, we'll get along just fine," Daddy said, sticking out his hand to shake.

The man took Daddy's hand and returned the introduction. "I'm James Quincy" he said, and then one by one introduced all the folks standing behind him. With the kids included, there were twenty-six in all. "We'll all work hard and try our best to make you good crops."

"Well, there's not a doubt in my head about that. Prayers have been answered both ways here, and I don't want any of y'all thinkin you've come here beholden anything to me. Besides that," Daddy said, putting his hand on mine and Jess's heads, "looks like my young'uns will finally have somebody to entertain them besides me. That's worth a year's wages all by itself!"

Mama had told me most of the folks we'd be meeting would have probably led a hard life. "Don't expect them to have extras and don't ask them why," she said sternly. "Just treat them like you would anyone else, and they'll appreciate it." I knew from the moment I saw them that Mama was right. Most their clothes were torn or patched and the shoes they wore, if they had any at all, were barely making it. All the croppers who had come were white people except for the Tolson family, who were Negroes. There was no mama with that family, just a daddy and two boys who were older and a girl who looked about my age. The girl's name was Sipsey, and even though I had tried to make her feel welcome, I could tell the new place and people made her feel shy.

Once we had all finished eating, Pastor Seth stood up to speak. "I wanted to put this off 'til after we had eaten, cause if you're like me you don't listen too well on an empty stomach," he

said laughing. "My friend Pastor Smoats used to come out where
y'all were stayin each Sunday afternoon and bring his message,
and weather permittin, I'll come out to Melrose after I finish in
town and do some stump preachin, bein as we'll all be a settin
outside. We all know how important it is to feed our body so it'll
keep going. It's just as important to feed our souls, you know.
Now, Winford thinks it'd be best for the women and children to
stay here at the gin while the men come out to the plantation to
help ready the place y'all will be stayin at. We'll make sure your
families are all cared for and we'll bring them out to you in a
couple a days. Another thing is, I know y'all have been workin for
other folks and through your dealings with them, you mighta found
'em hard to trust after awhile. I'm here to tell you Winford Taylor
ain't one of their kind. Also, through some circumstances that have
recently happened, Winford and his family have been richly
blessed by God, and he wants to share it with each and every one
of you. So if y'all will follow us over to the general store, we want
all of you to fit yourself with some work clothes, some dress
clothes, and a pair of shoes, and folks, it'll cost you nary a cent."

Once every one had been fitted, the men folk loaded
wagons with all the supplies they would need to fix up their new
homes at Melrose. "None of the cars are any different from the
next," Daddy told them once they got there. "Only the one on the
end there has doors on each side, and I want it to be used for
supplies and cookin," he said, pointing. After the tall grass had
been cut from around the cars, the men busied themselves with
making them a fit place for their families. Working side by side
without hardly a word, they moved from one rail car to the next,
patching each hole, making sure no wind or rain would be able to
reach them during a storm. After they were satisfied with that part,
they all moved to the pile of lumber and began sawing wood for
beds, tables, and benches to sit on. Wanting to help out, Jess and
me made ourselves useful toting boards and taking drinking water
to the men as they moved about from one task to the next. After
several hours of non-stop work, the men began gathering up the
tall grass they had cut earlier to line and soften the beds they had
made. After this was done, they brought out some of the benches

from the rail cars and sat them around a fire that was boiling water for coffee.

"It's been a good day, Mr. Winford," one of the men said. "When we left Huntsville, we was all a little scared, I reckon. Not knowin what to expect in a new place and all. We're mighty grateful to be here, though." As the others nodded in agreement.

"I'm real glad y'all are here," Daddy said. "I want y'all to know we are partners in what we're tryin to get accomplished here. I don't intend to get rich off of any of it. If we can take care of our families and still have a little jingle in our pockets for extras now and then, I reckon that'd make me happy enough. Pastor Seth had mentioned to everyone at the gin about me and my family being blessed, and that is true. I won't go into details about how all that came about, but I do want to say the main thing we'll be growin out here will be cotton, and I'm sure that don't surprise any of you. What will be different is when the crops are ready and picked, y'all will be paid cash money from the gin that me and Mr. Wiley own. All of the food and supplies, the stoves, even the mules and milk cows that will be brought here in the next few days are gifts. It all came from what God has given me or the folks from our church and community. None of it goes against your account. There won't be no accounts here. It makes no sense to me to keep a hard workin man down just cause he's in a different place in life than another might be." He said rising to his feet. "I like my coffee bout six o'clock every morning," Daddy said as several of the men sat wipin tears from their eyes. "I'll bring the breakfast."

It was several more days 'til things seemed fit to call for the croppers' families. Outhouses had to be dug, a corral built for the mules and milk cows, and two new stoves placed in the storage car for cooking up the meals. The last wagon that came brought a dozen setting hens for the new chicken house and also a stone Daddy had ordered for Ol' Doolah's grave. After Daddy and the deputy had finished what the sheriff asked them to do, they came back and buried Doolah a little distance from his house, where his wife Sootie and little girl Trixie had been buried years before. Doolah had mentioned Trixie to Jess and me more than once over the years. He talked about how smart and full of life she was. "I figured one day she be a teachin school somewhere if'n she woulda lived and been taught from books and such. It sho nuff bout kilt me when my baby girl left this world," Ol' Doolah would say each time. We never brought it up ourselves because we could tell how it always pulled on his heart so much, but from time to time something would happen to remind him and he'd tell us a story about her.

On our way home that day, we stopped at Doolah's grave and placed the stone Daddy had ordered. It read:

Doolah Samuel
Born 1828
Died March 15, 1906
"Never A More Gentle Soul"

Once the marker was in place, a quiet reverence swept over each of us and within moments tears started trickling down both my and Jess' face. After awhile, Daddy finally found a few words to comfort us in our sadness. "I think it'd be mighty nice for y'all to stop by and visit his grave from time to time. Maybe even drop off some of the treasures you find. I'm sure Ol' Doolah could tell y'all all about 'em."

Chapter 6

Melrose School

It wasn't long before Jess and I got to know each of the croppers' children by name. Most of them seemed to be the humble sort with only a couple who had to ever be called down from time to time by their parents. Even though there were other girls, they were either too young or old for me to play with much, so it was Sipsey and me who would become the very best of friends. We shared every secret and story we'd ever known with each other. There were also times Mama would let me invite her to stay over at our house. I think it touched Mama and Daddy both that Sipsey lived in this world without a mama of her own, and so they went out of their way to brag on her whenever she was around. Though she hadn't learned to read or write anything besides her name, she seemed to have a gift of remembering things better than anyone. Once when Mama invited her to sit in on our lessons, she had been able to cipher back every arithmetic problem she had seen worked. Mama referred to it as being gifted, and although Jess and me didn't really understand what that might mean at the time, we knew it must be good. We tried to be careful with what we gave Sipsey as far as clothes and such because we knew how the other children could become jealous and pick at her, and we didn't want to ever make her father feel short on the things he couldn't provide.

What we didn't know was that Mama had been taking Sipsey's unique giftedness to God in prayer for a while now. Asking him how she could possibly keep her in a regular learning situation without the other children feeling slighted. Then finally one day when mama quit putting off going through all of Ol' Doolah's belongings, it hit her square on the head. We were at his house, loading furniture and other things into the wagon that she thought might be useful to the croppers, when she grabbed her face as if something had shocked her. "My God, Winford, I've seen this place before," she said, startling us all.

"Why sure you have, Anna," Daddy answered, as if she were acting strangely.

"No, no, no; I mean I had a dream about it the other night," Mama explained. "Not like other dreams I've had from being too busy and such. This one was special. I wanted to remember it, but it was hidin from me 'til just now when I walked back outside and saw the open door. In my dream I was about eight months pregnant, and I was standin out here about where I am now. Ol' Doolah was there in the doorway and his little girl Trixie, the one who died, was standin by him. I'd never seen her, but in my dream I knew it was her. They were both standin there smiling at me, and then Doolah started motioning for me to come on inside. When I went in, the place was empty except for a few benches, and Doolah's little girl Trixie was now settin on one of 'em. When she saw me, she got up and walked over kinda shy like and handed me two beautiful little brass keys and said, 'My daddy said to give these to you. One is for this place and the other is a gift from Kate Shepard.' Then as she was walkin back to the bench to sit down, the door opened and I turned to see some of the croppers kids comin in. Once they were all seated, I looked back over to where Trixie had been settin, but it wasn't her anymore; it was Sipsey settin there. Winford," Mama said, beginning to cry, "God has answered my prayer, and I feel myself to be too short for what He wants me to do."

"Then you're in the right spot as far as God is concerned," Daddy said as he held Mama.

"But I'm still at a loss as to why I was with child," Mama said.

"Well, just give it some time," Daddy answered. "God'll clear up the muddy water, and when He does, it'll all make sense."

After the wagon was loaded and Mama had gathered her feelings, we headed around the bend, hoping the folks could make use of some of Ol' Doolah's stuff. "We'd be honored if'n y'all would all stay for supper," James said. He was usually the one who approached Daddy on everyone else's behalf. "We got us a mess a fish and my wife makes the best corn dodgers I ever et."

"We'd love to, James," Daddy said. "Besides, Anna here has somethin she wants to tell all a y'all," he said, turning to Mama, who slapped him on the arm in embarrassment. "Well, at least I *thought* she had something to share with y'all." He laughed.

Once everyone had finished eating, Mama did muster up the courage to talk. "I know this is plantin time. I can see ya all gettin the fields and garden patches ready for it. For years my daddy grew some a the finest cotton I've ever seen and some a the best food I've ever put in my mouth, right here on this plantation. Now I recon it's y'all's turn to do the same and be blessed by it. Anyway, if you don't mind, I wanted to visit ya with an idea, and then once you get through plantin, you can let me know if it suits you. God has given me a dream to start a school right over yonder in Ol' Doolah's house. But I got to tell ya the only teachin I've ever done was when I helped my Aunt Julia a little, years ago, and of course I been keepin my own children's lessons up since we moved out here. I'm willin to work around the chores, and come pickin' time for the cotton, we'll take a break, 'cause I know that's the cash crop. So y'all just think on that and let me know after everything's planted," Mama said, kinda stepping back.

"Miz Anna, I'm Isabel, James's wife, and I'd like to say a word if'n ya don't mind," she said. "There ain't a soul here can read but a speck, I reckon. And as far as ciphering goes, 'bout the only thing we know is what's owed to us fer the pound we picked. I never had any hopes a things gettin' better fer my young'uns neither, but since we moved here I done see'd charity like I ain't never see'd it before. If you're willin to teach, I'll back you up with my young'uns," Isabel said, with everyone else nodding in agreement. "I just got one favor to ask of ya. Come Sunday after Pastor Seth is done with us, could you spare a couple a hours workin with the grown folk?"

"Oh, my goodness, yes," Mama replied excitedly. "It would be my privilege to do just that!"

For the next several weeks I don't think I had ever seen Mama more excited about something in my whole life. Finally after the planting was over, her dream became reality when everyone gathered up around Ol' Doolah's place ready to outfit it for a schoolhouse. Knowing the women would want first dibs for cleaning and such, the men folk busied themselves outside making the benches and tables.

"We need to build some kinda desk for Miz Anna," James said after a while.

"And a proper chair fer her to set in, too," another piped in. Then, pointing his finger up a little like he had an idea, the second man motioned for James and the rest to follow. "There's good plank lumber in that ol' hen house yonder and them roostin poles will make fer some good legs, I bet."

"That's good thinkin," James said, walking over to the hen house.

"I'm glad I thought of it."

Within another hour or so, the men had fashioned a desk and a chair for Mama, which they took into the new school house. "Miz Anna," James said. "It ain't much and we still need to smooth the top off some, but we wanted to make you a proper place to set when you look over our young'uns work."

"My Lord," Mama said as she stepped back, almost beginning to squall. "It's like God has put just the right folks in place for this and not one detail has He overlooked." She then hugged each one of them.

That night, Mama had another dream, which she shared with us over breakfast the next morning. "I was ringin the school bell, and Ol' Doolah walked outta the woods with a big smile and handed me a newborn baby and said, 'Dat dream God done gave you is here, Miz Anna,' and then turned and walked away."

"Well, now," Daddy said, smiling at Mama. "I guess God has done cleared up that muddy water fer ya hadn't he?"

Not long after the place was fixed up and Mama had put all the school supplies in place, I raised the flag and Jess rang the bell for the very first time. We were surprised that not only did the children come, but their parents came as well, all dressed like they were going to church. Once they got up to where we were, James stepped forward. "Miz Anna, we been talkin these last two days, and we decided it was important fer us to come here for the start of this school and pray over you and what you're a doin here. We done told our young'uns what would happen if'n they start misbehaving, and I think we got 'em all scared to death bout that. But the main thing is, we all feel mighty blessed to have a chance at some schoolin, and we wanted to thank God fer it."

"That is a wonderful idea," Mama said. And with that, James and the others laid their hands on her and prayed.

Chapter 7

Sipsey

To my way of thinking, God sure didn't know what he was doing when it came time to divvy up the blessings, at least not for the first ten or so years of my life. For while others moved through the day with hardly a thought, I always sensed a cloud was following above me that was as black as my skin and stank like a pole cat. Although my mouth was quiet about these thoughts, it was my mind that was full of such notions. Once, when I did try telling my Granny Moss just how I felt, she let me know real quick that I ain't seen no hard times.

"Dem slavin days was hard times, girlie," Granny Moss would say. "Sun up til sundown we was workin for da man. Dey says I was born in '49 and by de time I was seven, I was in dem fields pickin dat cotton. Yes ma'am, I worked dem fields till dem Yankee soldiers come and says we ain't got to do it no mo, but here we is forty years later, still pickin dis cuss-ed cotton."

I understood what she was saying, of course, and I had it easy compared to my brothers, who spent most of their days out in the hot fields; I just thought there must be more to life than me toting water out to them and helping granny cook the meals. There were times when I escaped the dark corners I sat in for so long, like when I was playing with other children or on Sundays when Pastor Smoats would come out to where us croppers stayed to bring a message of hope.

"He's always with you," the preacher would say, "even though you don't see him, he's there wantin you to get to know him better." Pastor Smoats would also remind us about how God knows where each one of us is in life and how freedom has a different meaning to him than what it does to us. I didn't understand then a whole lot of what he was saying, but it did give me hope and as my daddy often said, "Hope is something you can hang your hat on when you ain't got nothin else."

Looking back, I realize how God had his hand on me the whole time, though. There were things He let me see during my young years that I kept strictly to myself— not from fear that others wouldn't believe me; rather, that I wasn't able to explain it in a way that could be understood. Like the time I was eight and was told to take some water out to the field for Daddy and them to drink. I could only carry the bucket just so far before I had to sit it down to change hands. Once when I had done that and was about to pick it up again, I looked up and saw the fields all full of Negroes hoeing the ground. They were from a different time. The clothes they wore were as ragged as I had ever seen, and I knew what I was seeing was from the slaving days Granny Moss had spoke about. Then as I stood there watching, they all began singing an old spiritual song: "Gawn break dem chains, gawn break dem chains; yes, my Lawd gawn break dem chains, gawn shine his sun, gawn shine his sun; yes, my Lawd gawn shine his sun." And as they sang, one of the men turned and smiled a big smile as if the song was a promise to only me and no one else. Then, just as suddenly as my mind seemed to grasp the full of it all, what I was seeing disappeared.

There was another such thing that happened to me when I was ten. Several months before, we had all been told we would be moving to a plantation in south Alabama near a town called Enterprise. I had a very vivid dream one night not long after Granny Moss had died. Her death had affected me tremendously because of the closeness I had had with her. In my dream, I was down by the creek visiting her grave. I had the sense that I was saying goodbye to her for the last time. When I finally found the strength to get up, I noticed an older black man and what I perceived to be his little girl standing there at the edge of the woods waiting for me. The old man was smiling and the little girl was motioning me too hurry up and come on, like she had something she wanted to show me. As I made it to the edge of the woods and looked out into the field, they were no longer there, which was disappointing to me. But then as I looked up into the sky, which had been dark and gloomy when I first went into the woods, it was now clearing up, and the rays of the sun began shining through, making it the most beautiful day I had ever seen.

It wasn't long before all these things would come together and lift the darkness I had carried for so long in my soul. God would also deal with the anger I had over the death of my Granny Moss. It was an anger that was mostly feelings and hard to put into words. She was the closest thing I had to a mama. I had been told that my real mama had died giving birth to me, and in my little-child mind, I figured I had killed her somehow. Now, God had seen fit to punish me by taking my granny away. I felt like I was left with nothing. There was Daddy, of course, but the bond I had with Granny Moss was different, and now it was gone. I felt surely that my life was over in spite of the dream God had given me. I didn't want to move away, either. I didn't want to leave the place where I had spent time with Granny. If memories were all I could have, let me have them here, in the shack we lived in, at the creek where we washed clothes, and in the woods where we gathered roots and berries. I didn't want to move, and I surely didn't want to be around those folks Pastor Smoats said we'd be meetin. I thought about running away and hiding in the woods, but I knew what kind of punishment I'd get if they found me. I also knew it would be hard to make it on my own, and besides that, I would be scared. There was a wampus cat out there somewhere, a big black panther that always showed up this time of year. I had heard it scream before, and it sounded just like a woman screaming, and I didn't want any more of it. After thinking about that, I decided it'd be best to go on with all the others; besides, the man we had been cropping for had a bad habit of reminding my family we were colored folk and lucky to be a part of what he had – something that never sat well with my daddy anyway.

Chapter 8

Darkness Lifted

When we got to Enterprise, I remember Mr. Winford and his family waiting to meet us all at the station. When his little girl, Janie, saw me she waved like she was expecting me, but I just kinda put my head down like I didn't see her. I stuck real close to my daddy, and several times he had to peel me off of his leg just so he could walk. I sat right up next to where he sat when we ate, and it was only during the prayer that I dared to look at folks. When the preacher stood to speak and said the women and children were going to stay at the mill while the men went somewhere to get our living places fixed up, my stomach knotted up just like it did when I heard that wampus cat scream. I was scared to death and didn't like the idea of being away from my daddy and brothers. Finally, Miz Isabel, who had good sense and had stood beside me at Granny Moss's funeral, came over and asked if it wouldn't be a good idea if my brother Spookie (we called him that because his eyes bugged out like he was scared) could stay with her until we got to our new place, and that suited Daddy because he knew I wasn't about to let go of him if he didn't settle my mind on the matter.

As it turned out, staying at the mill wasn't nearly as bad as I thought it'd be. Pastor Seth was always playing games or telling us kids Bible stories, and the folks from church were bringing us food and sweets. But the thing that held my mind even more than candy was the new store-bought clothes and shoes I had gotten. I've never been so proud of anything in my whole life. I remember waking up each morning and first thing checking to make sure my new dress, with the pretty flowers on it, was still there. I had mostly worn old hand-me-downs that Pastor Smoats's church would send from time to time, and then I had some flour sack dresses that Granny Moss had made me; those I'd wear on hot days when I was out carrying water. When we were at the store, Janie had come over to show me where the clothes for girls were, and because she kept on talking, I finally figured I might as well talk back, and after awhile I warmed up to her a little. She told me about the place we'd be living once they got everything done, and promised she would come out to see me.

That Sunday after we had all been fed, Pastor Seth had several wagons brought by to take us out to our new homes. Me and Spookie and some others rode in a wagon driven by a big white boy named Benny. I never could figure out what he was a swatting at the whole time we were riding. I didn't see any bugs, and I couldn't place the reason for him hollering out every now and then, either. Finally, after a good hour's ride, we made it to our new home. Daddy was there waiting for us and gave me one of the biggest hugs he had ever given me. I was glad to see him, too, and held his hand as he showed us all around the place. "Mr. Taylor done fixed us up real nice, chillun," Daddy said. "He gave us that rail car yonder to live in. Folks from his church done stocked us with food, and we got two stoves in that last car for da women to do all the cookin on. He also says we don't owe him nothin for any of it, and to top it off, when da cotton comes in, we's gwana have some cash money."

I could tell by the way daddy was acting that he was relieved from the notion that we might not be treated right again. There was a pep in his walk now that I hadn't seen in a long time.

After everyone seemed settled in, Pastor Seth called us all together for prayer and wanted us to join him for something special. "I only want a speck of your time today, 'cause you all deserve to be with your families," he said, motioning us to gather. Then once he said a few words, we all headed down to the creek where Janie and her family were waiting. "I've known this girl all her life," Pastor Seth said once he and Janie had waded down into the water. "A couple months ago, she asked God to come into her heart, and we are here to celebrate that decision today. Janie, do you promise to always give God a place in your life and show others how to do the same?" he asked. Janie nodded and then Pastor Seth said, "then I baptize you my sister, in the name of the Father and of the Son and of the Holy Ghost," and with that, he laid her into the water and raised her back up again. The whole thing was very moving to me, seeming to plant a seed in my own heart that would find a way to grow even in the darkness.

That night, laying in bed I thought a lot about Granny Moss and held tightly to something she had given me when I was but four years old. It was a little rag doll made from scraps of cloth left from some sewing she was hired to do. When I unwrapped it from the old brown paper back then, I remember Granny saying, 'she'll haft to be yo friend when I's busy, cause I cain't be's turnin around every time you goes to hollerin fo me gul.' That was nothing but talk though, cause I never could remember a moment she ignored me.

Now though, I needed her more than ever. I was uneasy and wishing she could have made the trip with me to this place. It seemed to hold a lot of promise, but I wondered what she would make of it, and felt it was cheating to embrace something without her winking at it. I remember right before they laid her down Pastor Smoats saying her work was done here, and it was time for her to rest and enjoy the promises God had set aside for her. It was hard for me to understand that. She was the biggest part of my life, and I didn't want her going off and enjoying anything without me. Besides I knew there'd never be anyone else who would turn around for me when I hollered for them. At least not the way she always had.

I thought and fretted about these things off and on for the rest of the week until the following Sunday when Janie and her family came out to visit us for church. Before the service, I saw Miz Anna and Mr. Winford talking to my daddy off to the side, with Janie standing there with them. Daddy was nodding his head all along and every now and then, Janie would look over at me. After awhile, Miz Anna and Janie started motioning for me to come over to where they were.

"Sipsey, we were wonderin if you'd like to come visit with Janie for a couple a days," Miz Anna asked. "Your daddy said it would be fine with him and we'd love to have you."

I looked up at Daddy, who nodded his head at me. "You go on, girl, and play with Janie for awhile. You been workin hard and need the rest," Daddy said, teasing like.

The invitation to Janie's had settled my fretting and thoughts about Granny Moss, and by the time we had all gathered up outside the rail cars to hear Pastor Seth preach, my mind was freed up for what he had to say.

"I'm so glad to be here," he started. "This ain't Heaven, but it's exactly where God wants us to be. That trip y'all made from Huntsville, in your minds it was probably the longest trip you had ever taken. Not knowin what to expect, that can scare anybody. To be honest with you, not knowin what to expect sometimes scares me as much as it does everyone else. It's like death. We can hear about heaven our whole life, but when it comes down to it and we're actually dyin, we begin to wonder if all those things we heard about the place are true. Well, think about this: Have you ever known anyone who went there and came back 'cause they didn't like it as much as this place? No, I don't think so. As a matter of fact, I'll guarantee you if you had the chance to talk to someone you knew here on this earth and who is up there with God right now, they'd tell you they ain't about to leave the place, but they'll be in line to meet you when you make it up there.

Folks, I know we don't like change. I know we don't like to lose those people we are close to, but up there in Heaven is where our life truly begins, and it won't never end. Folks, my mama died when I was twelve years old, and I was so mad at God for letting her die I didn't know what to do, and I stayed that way for quite a spell. Then a couple of years later when I was livin with my Granny Pate, her twin sister died. I knew it was grievin her to no end cause they was as close as close could be. One mornin real early when I was outside gatherin some kindling, I saw Granny through the window down on her knees with her hands lifted up like she was handin something off to somebody. At breakfast that morning, I noticed she was in much better spirits about everything. Then about a year later, she was talkin to someone who lived down the road from us who had lost a child several years before. 'It's not good, you holdin on to 'em like that,' my granny said. 'It'll kill ya.'

"It's been killin me,' the woman said, "but I don't know what to do about it."

"You got to let go of 'em," Granny said. "You got to hold 'em up and give 'em to God. If you can find the courage to do that, he'll give 'em back to you in a way you never dreamed of."

"Folks, I don't know if you're holdin on to someone you may have lost or to some hard feelins you might have against someone. But it'll kill ya if you don't let go of it," Pastor Seth said. "So when you're in your private place talkin to God, hold those things up to him and see what he gives ya back in its place. I did that with my mama and not only did my joy for life return, but God also began pourin out his blessins on me, and he ain't stopped yet."

That night after I had gone home with Janie and we were about to head off for bed, Pastor Seth hugged me and said, "Sipsey, I'm so glad you came to live down here. I'm gonna write Pastor Smoats and tell him that you and your daddy and brothers are all getting along just fine." Then when I was lying in bed, I could still hear the grown folks talking. "God laid that message on my heart today, Winford. He does that kinda thing sometimes. He'll arrange it so my words will touch that person who has gotten all of their feelins and thoughts messed up over something. If it's a youngun and something bad happens, they don't have the power to reason through it all, and even when they're older and things happen, they get mad at God and hold a grudge. Either way, those chains are mighty hard to get loose from. I just wish I had told 'em they was welcome to come and talk or pray with me, cause sometimes those things can stay hid inside ya till God puts his finger on it and then he wants someone to be there for you when it all comes up."

After hearing the pastor say these things, I remembered his sermon that day and began to pray, trying to let go of my granny like he preached about, but I had such a heavy feeling of sadness come over me all of a sudden that I didn't know what to do. The vision I had about the slaves singing came back to me —"Gawn break dem chains, gawn break dem chains," and then in the middle of it all, I heard Granny Moss's voice as clear as day say, "Sipsey,

yo mama didn't die cause a you, baby. She was already sick."
When I heard that in my head, I did something that I was
embarrassed about for years. I ran to where Pastor Seth was sitting,
buried my head in his shoulder, and squalled for what seemed like
an hour. Here I was a black girl, so shy I would hardly talk to folks,
and I was crying on this white man's shoulder, and in front of other
folks, too.

He held me through every bit of it, though, all the time
saying, "You just cry it all out, take as long as you need, we ain't
goin nowhere." When I finally got through, Miz Anna helped me
wash my face, got me some water to drink, and then tucked me
into the bed.

My life was never the same after that happened. The
darkness that had once hovered around me was now gone. Slowly,
over the next few weeks and months, I became a whole different
person. I would sing and hum all through the day when I was by
myself, but even more so, I found myself laughing about things. I
laughed at myself, and I laughed at other folks. I laughed when it
didn't make any sense, and I laughed when folks put an odd look
on their face because of my laughing! It didn't hardly take
anything to set me off, and Janie, whenever she was around, would
be right there with me laughing, too.

Chapter 9

Called to Teach

I had never met many folks like the Taylors. They were kind and honest and never held themselves above us croppers nor treated me or my family as second class because we were Negro. Daddy had long since earned respect from the other croppers because of how hard he worked with them, and Mr. Winford earned mine from how he would pitch in when there were things to be done. He also made sure we had what we needed as far as extras, and more than once made special trips into town if someone needed to be looked at by the doctor.

It seemed our lives had changed for the better. When the school was started by Miz Anna, the children and grown folks alike grabbed hold of the lessons she taught like they were drowning and couldn't get enough air. After the first cotton came in and all the families were paid, I remember how everyone got together for a meeting one night and decided they would give a portion of what they'd earned to buy new books and supplies. "It ain't fair them footin the bill for everything," one man said. "We got to do our part." He was right, of course, and between the whole lot of us we put in over fifty dollars that first year. Eventually, we built and started our own library, a little room which was added onto our school house. Once it was finished and even though it was hardly filled with books, Miz Anna allowed each of us to take turns being the librarian. It was about the most exciting thing any of us had ever done, and we figured we were just as high and mighty as that Mr. Teddy Roosevelt was, sitting up there in his big ol' white house. Then a little later when Pastor Seth finally got around to his quarterly report to his congregation about all of our doings at Melrose School, the church folk got to sending us books by the box full, making us all feel like we were really stepping in high cotton.

Miz Anna took the time to find out what particular things interested each one of us the most and made an effort to get information on those subjects. At the same time, she stressed the importance of how we should balance our education out. "It'll make you well rounded," she said. "And practice reading out loud to each other. That way you'll know how to pronounce the words better." She also worked with us on how to write letters to folks. We'd pick someone from Pastor Seth's church and let them know what we had been learning in school. We were also reminded that we should thank them for how they had helped take care of us from the moment we first arrived in Enterprise.

What with my lessons, chores, and playing with Janie, I hardly ever took the time to pray. It bothered me knowing that during all the good that had come to me in the last several years, that I hadn't taken much time to thank God for it. Even though it might have been the Taylors and the good folks from Pastors Seth's church who had showed us so much charity, it was God who had planned everything out for us. He had brought us out of a bad situation in Huntsville and given us hope and a future, just like he talked about in the book of Jeremiah. One night, I confessed my short sightedness to Him and promised to pay more attention to where His hand was in my life, and where it might be leading me. Then, not long after I prayed that prayer, I asked Pastor Seth to baptize me like he had done Janie when we had first come to Melrose. It was in the spring of 1912, and I was seventeen years old.

Although Janie and I had shared all kinds of notions about where we wanted to go in life, we now found ourselves to be coming of age. Our thoughts and actions had matured over time, and we both made our futures a matter of prayer, knowing that God would direct our paths. Miz Anna had spoken to us on more than one occasion about continuing our education at college, and on my behalf, she had corresponded several times with Mr. Booker T. Washington of Tuskegee Institute.

The thought of leaving my family, my best friend Janie, and all the other things I was used to was scary, but I was older now and had much more faith in knowing God was opening a door for me. Besides that, Janie would be starting college in Troy not more than a week after I was, and the support and expectations we both had from everyone at Melrose only confirmed what we already knew in our hearts, which was that we must pursue our dreams of becoming teachers.

Chapter 10

College Bound

Daddy had arranged for Benny to take Sipsey and me into Troy by buggy, a trip that would take a good six hours one way with the horses being stopped for feed and water. It was cheaper than a train ticket, and Benny, who had gotten into some trouble several nights before, needed the money to avoid the jail time he would receive if his fine and court costs were not paid.

"I hate to do it to y'all," Daddy said, "makin you take such a long trip with him and all, but I'm gonna need him next week and he won't do me a bit of good settin up there in that jail house."

From the story I was told, Benny had been arrested at the carnival for failure to pay for an exhibit he participated in. He was also charged with disorderly conduct for the same event. A crowd of folks had gathered around a fortune teller who would charge twenty five cents to tell someone's future. Benny was the first to volunteer from the crowd and began arguing with the woman about the prophecies she had predicted for him. After several minutes, she finally gave up and began demanding her money. Benny refused to pay, citing the fact that with her powers of mind, she should have known from the very get-go that he was flat broke.

Once we had gotten underway, Sipsey and I sat in the back seat chatting about nothing in particular and laughing every so often when Benny would holler out or start swatting at invisible things. Of course, we always covered our mouths when it was Benny who'd gotten us tickled. We knew he was cursed with these peculiarities and didn't want to add embarrassment to all the other worries he might have on his mind. About half way to Troy, we had a hard rain come up on us, so Benny, who was not covered by the buggy top, pulled under a large oak tree to wait it out. After sitting for a few minutes, I noticed he pulled out some cookies he had taken from the gin that morning and started eating one after the other while chasing them with big gulps of water. Benny had a huge appetite, and was teased by the other workers for the amount of food he devoured during lunch. "No wonder all your dogs run away from home; there ain't enough scraps left to feed a blow fly once you're done," they would joke. They also learned very quickly to never leave any of their snacks lying around for fear he'd steal them for his own consumption.

After thirty minutes or so, the rain let up and Benny was eager to get going again, so he snapped the reins and started the horses out at a fast trot in hopes of making up for the time we had lost. We had gone only one or two miles when he once again pulled the buggy to a stop and began tearing sheets out of a writing tablet that Daddy had kept his notes in. Then, he jumped down off the buggy and with a quick step, he headed towards the woods, hollering over his shoulder that he'd be right back. Sipsey and I took this time to stretch our legs and eat some of the fried chicken we had packed ourselves for lunch. Some time had passed since Benny had walked off and we started worrying about him. The weather was ripe for snakes and the place he had headed was near a river, which was known to draw its share of the legless reptiles. After several more minutes, I decided it'd be best to check on him, but not wanting to bring embarrassment to any predicament he might be in, I entered the woods a ways down from where Benny had gone in. After stepping about gingerly, I finally made out the top of his head as he was still squatting with his bottom hanging over the edge of the river bluff, swift water running not more than seventy feet below him.

"They put somethin in them cookies. I heard him shout out real angry like. "And now I been settin so long I can't move my legs."

Apparently, the men at the gin had laced the cookies with a laxative and placed them in full view, knowing Benny would grab them the first chance he got.

Being confused about the situation, I wasn't sure what I should do: Offer him a hand or just leave, hoping he'd manage his own way out? Then, before I could make up my mind, he began rocking forward trying to grab hold of an old lightered stump that was in front of him but just out of his reach. After about four or five good rocks, he managed to catch hold of it. He then made it about half way up to a standing position when the stump was pulled up and out of the ground, throwing poor Benny backwards and over the bluff. The slope down to the river was steep, and he rolled end over end for several turns until finally his body righted itself out straight. Then he was into a quick slide, trying to grab any sapling or vine that would slow him down. By the time he reached the river bank below, he had been eaten up by briars from the top of his head down to his shins, with only his ankles spared because of the britches that were hanging around them. Bare-bottomed and exhausted he stood to his feet, looking back up the bluff.

"Son of a jack horse!" he finally yelled while slapping his leg. "That dern fortune women should a warned me about this!"

Thank God, Benny never saw me and when he started washing himself in the river, I broke and ran for the buggy. Halfway there, I fell into a fit of laughter like I had never done before. I stumbled and fell several times from the tears that blinded my eyes, and by the time I had gotten back to the buggy, I fainted from the lack of air I was able to take in. It was a good ten minutes before I could even begin to get words out to Sipsey, who was by then more contagious with my laughter than able to discern what little sense my story was making. When poor Benny came walking up, soaking wet and with his shirt torn, I had to run off a piece to finish getting it out of my system. But even then I found myself burying my head in laughter more than a dozen times before we made it to Troy.

Chapter 11

A Curse Broken

My ribs were still sore from all the laughing I had done on our trip, and now reading Sipsey's letter made me hurt when I'd get to some funny part she had written. In spite of all the delays with Benny, we managed to make it for her departure on the Tuskegee-bound train. Now, only six days later, she was detailing every fact of her new life to me. I couldn't help but think of how far she had come over the years: once a shy little girl who hung to her father's britches leg to now, a confident almost eighteen-year-old lady who would look me in the eye when she spoke. And then there was her giftedness. She had the most amazing ability to pick up on and remember any subject we were studying at Melrose School. Now, here she was living away from family and friends, yet so giddy about college and all the people she was meeting.

I was right excited myself; classes would begin for me in a week and I couldn't wait. I would be living with Aunt Julia, Daddy Jack's sister, about a half mile from Troy Normal School. Aunt Julia had retired from this very school as a teacher, and she was helpful to me in choosing my subjects and professors. "Some of the teachers can be downright overbearing," she warned. "They try to impress you with their intellect, and it's about as impressive as one of those new horseless carriages you see stuck in the mud. It'll get you nowhere quick," she added with a chuckle. With Aunt Julia's wise counsel, I settled on mathematics, English, world history, and Christian religion for my first term.

Even though I enjoyed all my new classes, it was the religion class that was my favorite. It was taught by a Reverend Clayton McLean, a delightful and humorous man who also pastored one of the local churches in Troy. After he introduced himself, I remember his addressing us in a stern voice: "I have two rules and I expect you to abide by them. Rule number one is *do not be late for my class!* I like tardiness about as much as a Yankee likes grits," he said without blinking. "Rule number two is *never let me catch you sleepin in my class!* If you fall asleep while I am teachin, I will consider that an insult to my integrity. I am from Mississippi, and God has placed me here to try and raise you folks up to the same level of standin that we all share in that great state. Now, since I have gotten your attention and you have such serious looks on your faces, I take it that you either wholeheartedly believe what I have just uttered, or you think I am crazy and don't want to hurt my feelins with your laughter," he said, slowly gazing around the room. "Well, I am crazy!" he hollered, making us all jump about two feet from our desks, "and before you finish my class, you will be, too!"

His lessons from the Bible were not the kind you usually heard coming from the pulpit. They delved much deeper into symbolism and opened up what he referred to as our imaginations. "It's through our Holy imagination that we hear and see our Lord," he said, "and it functions best when our head and our heart have no chasm between them. Now, I want you to listen to me for a minute, so I can explain a little bit of what you will be learnin in this class. When Jesus told his disciples in John, Chapter 14 that when he left them, the Holy Spirit would come, this was not only for their benefit, but because he wanted all people of every tribe and nation to be able to experience the same kind of relationship with him that only the few who were close to him could enjoy. For you see, Jesus our Lord, choosing to become a man was bound by time and geographical location, and he knew it would be this way until his work was finished. But! Now through the person of the Holy Spirit he is able to fellowship with all who seek his presence, no matter that we aren't with him physically.

Now I don't want you to feel threatened in thinkin that I am here to disagree with what your preacher or Sunday school teacher has already taught you. It also doesn't imply that what you will hear in this class is a new theory or that what I'm teachin is not biblically based; it just means you may have never been challenged to think about these concepts. And I can promise you this: God wholeheartedly delights in those who search him out. You take Job, for instance. He went from being someone who was acquainted with ritual to someone who knew our creator in an intimate way even sayin in the thirty fourth chapter of the Book of Job, 'I had heard of who you were, but now I have seen your face.' It was because of his pressing into God for answers that Job was able to know God in a way that was not revealed through religion and ritual alone. Quite honestly, I detest the word *religion*," Reverend Clayton said, while walking between our desks.

"To me, it conjures up thoughts of Pharisee-like regulations that we must endure in order to find the Outer Court of our God. Now make no mistake; I will teach you the origins of the Christian faith and how the church as we know it evolved, but I would be doin you the most horrific injustice if I did not impress on you what changes our Lord was intimately yearning for when the veil that separated the people from His presence in the Holy of Holies was torn from top to bottom the day He was crucified."

Besides all the laughter Reverend Clayton brought among us that day, I found he was right. For many of the things he said I had never thought about, but my heart agreed that it was all true. I also knew that I would begin enjoying a freedom in God like I had never experienced before. On Mondays and Thursdays the three-hour class he taught seemed as if it were over in fifteen minutes. Of course, I would study the notes I had taken from each of his classes and usually spend extra time on homework projects he asked us to do.

One such assignment we had was to list what symbolisms we found in the story of Samson from the Book of Judges. I had heard that story many times, but other than knowing that Samson was the strongest man who ever lived, I couldn't make head nor tails of what he stood for. I was relieved to find my classmates were just as confused as I was.

"Samson," Professor Clayton remarked, while peeling an apple, "is a very interestin character. I confess I wrestled with his story for quite a spell tryin to figure out what it was God wanted me to see. It wasn't until later on, when I was fastin and prayin over something totally different that he gave me the answer I had been lookin for. I think He did it that way so that my mind would be out of the way on that subject, *and* so I would have no doubt where the answer came from. Now, as for your assignment, I honestly didn't expect you to come up with any real answers, but I knew if I gave you this you would not soon forget what I am about to share with you. If you will recall, Samson was deceived by his wife Delilah and then bound and taken into captivity by the Philistines. This was only possible once his hair was cut, which took away all of his great strength. Then, being bound and in a weakened state, his eyes were gouged out by his enemies, makin him blind. With no longer a way to see, he was led by others into a life of forced servitude. Class, what happened to Samson is a perfect picture of the deception of sin and what it will do to you. First, it will make you weak. Then, it will make you blind. Then!" He said pausing "It will make you a slave.

Now, I want each one of you to embrace the symbolisms of this story as you go about your day. Think on them, pray about them, and most importantly do not forget them. I also want to remind you of this: Samson's strength was not in his hair but in his commitment to God, which was actually made for him by his parents. And his hair was merely the outward expression of this commitment. The second thing I want you to realize is that it was not my intellect that came up with the symbolisms of this story. It was God who showed me these things, and He is just as willin to share these kinds of truths with each one of you. All you have to do is make your OWN COMITTMENT," he said, pausing to write it on the chalk board. "to meet with Him, on a regular basis. And by doing this! You will begin to find His strength and direction for your life."

Paying attention in class was never a problem for me. The things we covered were always interesting, and I usually walked out wishing the class had lasted another hour or so. Toward the end of the term, something happened to me that I will never forget. We had been covering the importance of forgiveness, and every night before going to sleep, I would ask God to show me where I may have faulted someone in my thoughts or actions.

After one such prayer and with nothing being impressed on me, I went on to bed looking forward to the extra rest I would get with the next day being a Saturday. Now, like most folks, I had never paid much attention to my dreams. None of them, if I could remember them at all, made much sense to me anyway, but that night was different. This one was so vivid and powerful that I wrote it down the moment I awoke the next morning. The dream started out with me standing in a huge room with caskets placed on tables. There were fifteen or twenty of them and I knew that each one of them held the body of an ancestor who had died long before my time. I was amazed at what I was seeing, and noticed that on top of each casket was a book about that person's life. While I was taking all of this in, I turned to look across the room and saw Daddy Jack lying on a table, dead. He was not in a casket, but he had one of those books placed across his chest. Then all of a sudden, my mother was in the dream. She timidly walked up to Daddy Jack, then reached to open his book; but just as she touched it, Daddy Jack started kicking at her real hateful-like and wouldn't allow her to see what was written. I remember how disappointed I was about the whole thing, and I stood trying to comfort Mama, who was by then filling the entire room with great sobs. Knowing that I had to do somethin to stop her anguish, I reached to square up her face with mine and to tell her I would open the book, but when I did this, I realized it was not her face I held in my hands; it had become my brother Jessup's.

I woke up startled and confused. I had never had such a vivid dream in my entire life, and I knew without a doubt there was something God wanted me to know here. I was anxious about the meaning and I spent half the day trying to come up with something that made sense. Finally, after realizing that the whole thing was beyond me, I surrendered it to God. He had given me the dream and I figured in good time he would also reveal to me what it meant.

Then one morning several days later and during my prayer time, I had a memory come back to me that I had forgotten about for years. It had happened in Troy when I was about six years old and we were at a family cemetery where relatives would gather to picnic and to clear the place of weeds and tall grass that had grown up since our previous visit. Daddy Jack, who was there with us, walked off a little piece by himself and stared at some graves that were away from the others. He talked some as he stood there, but he was too far away for me to make out what he was saying. I thought he must be touched in the head a little for doing that. I also remember thinking, "He spends more time speakin to dead folks than he ever did to me." Now as the memory came back, I stood there once again just as I had done that day. The unspoken words I had said to myself were as clear as if I'd heard them five minutes before. When I relived them, this time I had a deep conviction in my heart that I had previously sat in judgment of Daddy Jack. After being confronted with that, I sat there, my eyes welling up with tears, and asked God to forgive me for what I had done. I also wished I could ask Daddy Jack to forgive me for the thoughts I had about him that day, but knowing he was gone, it would have to be up to God to let him know how I felt, and I wasn't quite so sure how those kinds of things worked in Heaven.

When I had gotten a little older, I learned that the graves Daddy Jack had stood beside belonged to his mother and a sister, with his sister dying in some kind of accident many years ago. I had overheard someone speaking about the tragedy once, but the memory had grown murky, and I could recall only bits and pieces. I knew Aunt Julia would know the details, so I asked her when evening came and we did our usual porch settin. She always claimed her mind was clearer with a cool breeze and a good dip of snuff, anyway.

"Your Daddy Jack was just a boy and still livin at Melrose," Aunt Julia said. "Course by then, me, Ouida and Lois had all married and moved off to different places and was raisin our young'uns and such. Now Papa, who was my daddy, brought Jack and our youngest sister Bella, and Mama over here to Troy for a visit with his brother and to do some huntin and hog killin. It was winter time and that was when they would stock up on their meat for the year. I remember hearin that Bella and Mama stayed at the house that day while the rest of the women went on to town to pick up some things for cookin. Mama was pregnant with twins and was feelin poorly. Bella was left to tend to her the best she could and your Daddy Jack was made to stay and watch the fire the men had goin in the smoke house.

Well Jackie, as we sometimes called him for sport, was fit to be tied over that. He was already mad cause Papa wouldn't let him go off and fight the Yankees with his brothers and now he wouldn't let him go with the men folk huntin.

When Bella, who was bout five then, came out towards the privy, Jackie talked her into watchin the fire awhile so he could go off a piece in the woods to shoot at some squirrels he'd seen that mornin. He gave her a nickel and told her to poke that fire ever so often and to add a little wood every now and then to keep it goin. He then went on to try out his luck. About an hour or so passed when he heard some awful screamin comin from towards the house and ran back as fast as he could. When he got there, he found Bella all burnt up from nearbout head to toe and Mama kneelin down beside her, touchin what was left of her hair.

They stopped someone on the way into town and the doctor was fetched out to the house. Liniment was put on Bella night and day for over a week, but she didn't make it. Mama lost the babies, too. She said that when she heard Bella screamin, she looked out the window and when she made it to the door, she jumped the steps wantin to get to her as quick as she could. She landed hard and must a shook herself up on the inside. Papa had Bella buried out at the Griffith Cemetery, and when Mama died, she was to be buried next to Bella. Course Papa lived on ten years past her and got married again. That's why he's buried outside of Enterprise with his second wife. You know your Daddy Jack never got over the guilt of what he had done that day. It changed him. He was bout ten when it happened. Up til then he would laugh and stay in all kinda mischief, but once that happened, you never saw him in much conversation. I guess it takes Heaven to straighten them kinda things out, cause after that happened, he never was the same on this earth."

"My Lord," I thought to myself. "What an awful, terrible thing to have to live through." I realized then why Daddy Jack had stood talkin to those graves. I also understood to a certain point why he acted the way he did towards me and Jess. His feelings must have been all frozen up inside him. It was sad to me on both accounts, and I didn't know which was worse — the accident that happened that day or the fact that Daddy Jack had been burdened with the guilt all those years. I was like Aunt Julia in one respect, though, and was hoping that those kinds of things get straightened out when someone enters the Heavenly realms. I figured it was probably easy for those who show some reverence to God while they're here on earth. The problem was I never saw any of that from Daddy Jack while he was living in this world. It bothered me for his sake, especially since I had been shown the importance of forgiveness. That night, I talked to God about it for a long time. I told him I loved Daddy Jack, and if he didn't know it already, I wanted him to somehow know that I did. I also wanted him to know that what happened that day when he was a boy wasn't the end of Bella and those babies; it was a new beginning for them and this time it would have no end.

After my prayer that night, I really thought that'd be the end of it as far as Daddy Jack and I were concerned. I still thought about the dream off and on because I had never had another make such a mark on me. There were still parts of it that made no sense, but I resisted trying to figure them out. Whenever I did, it only made my thoughts get all scrambled.

Then one morning in Professor Clayton's church while he was praying, I had a picture pop up in my head. It was of a big sword like one of those Roman soldiers would have used. I knew what it was because I had seen a drawing in my history book. Nobody was holding the sword, but it had blood on it like it had been used in a fight or something. It kinda scared me. I knew swords were used for hurting folks, and with all the blood on it, I figured I must have injured somebody really bad with that sharp tongue of mine. I finally dismissed that picture and my thoughts on it, figuring I'd deal with it all later. We were about to have communion, and I wanted to pay attention to what was being said. The way they did communion at this church, folks would come up to the altar and pray for a moment, confessing their sins. Professor Clayton and his wife Mary would stand at the front, being available for anyone if they needed additional prayer. Then once you had prayed, you would break off a piece of bread and dip it in the wine, looking up at a large cross on the wall.

When I came up to the altar and knelt down, I had no particular prayer in mind, but not wanting to look like a heathen by getting up too fast, I stayed there looking out the corner of my eye to see when others might rise up. The two ladies beside me seemed to be taking forever with their confessions, so I finally closed my eyes as well and when my mind was settled, that same picture of the sword came back to me — but this time it came with words: "You need to forgive your grandfather" is what I heard plain as day. I continued to kneel there, stunned. I knew God was talking bout Daddy Jack, but I had no idea why I needed to forgive him for anything. What had happened to Daddy Jack occurred when he was a boy, and that was a long time before I was born. Then as I asked God what I needed to forgive him for, he put up a whole lot of pictures of Daddy Jack's life for me at one time. I knew what they meant the second I saw them. God was showing me how the accident had affected Daddy Jack, not only when it happened but as he grew up. The guilt he felt had choked the life out of him. He was unable to forgive himself, much less believe someone could ever love him after what he'd done. As he got older and allowed certain folks into his life, he was still apt to keep the closest ones at a distance. I saw this much for myself, and what I hadn't seen I had heard stories of.

There was only one other child besides my mama. It was Uncle Sal, who had spent most of his life livin off hard liquor. From what I had heard, after Granny May died with the fever, Daddy Jack was real hard on him growin up. Made him go to the fields and work even when they had company come for picnics and such, and on occasion, had even beat him in fits of rage. Sal was twelve years older than Mama and died when I was about three. I also remembered the grief Mama went through when Daddy Jack died. She felt cheated from not having the kinds of words spoken over her that she needed to hear when she was growing up.

After the pictures disappeared, I got up and went to Miz Mary. She could tell something was wrong, because my lip was quivering and tears were beginning to fill my eyes. "Miz Mary," I said, "God just told me I need to forgive my grandfather, but my mind is crossways over the whole thing." I then went on to tell her about the sword picture and the other pictures I had seen. I also told her a little about the dream I had had awhile back.

"Janie, what God is showin you is what the Bible talks about in the Old Testament. What happened to your grandfather has caused a generational curse in your family and God is givin you the opportunity to cut that curse with his blood, not only for your sake, but for all those who descended from your grandfather's seed. It will be done the moment you forgive him, and I couldn't think of a better time to do it than at communion." I nodded my head in agreement and then said a little prayer forgiving Daddy Jack for the distance he had showed us. After I took the bread and wine, Miz Mary said, "Remember, what we bind here on earth we bind in Heaven, and what we loose here on earth, we loose in Heaven."

That afternoon while lying on the bed, I thanked God for allowing me to stand up for my family on the whole matter and even for forgiving Daddy Jack, someone I had learned to love even after his death. The dream, the pictures, and even the words God had spoken made me feel humble. He had chosen me, a sinner full of foolishness, to extend forgiveness to someone. Now, I didn't know exactly what it meant for the living when a curse like that is broken, but I felt for sure that Daddy Jack was somehow set loose that day. Just the thought of him getting to see those he loved reminded me of the story of Joseph seeing his brothers after all those years. They had sold him into slavery a long time before, but Joseph, full of forgiveness and love, held no ill will towards any of them. I pictured Daddy Jack seeing that same kind of love and forgiveness in his sister Bella the moment he finally saw her in Heaven.

Chapter 12

The Perfect Gift

It had been almost four months since I had been home. Our Christmas break had started, and I was eager to see everyone, including Sipsey. She had made it home a few days before I did, and when my train pulled into Enterprise, she stood waiting on the platform with Mama, Daddy, and Jess. Jess, I noticed, had half an eyebrow missing. I found out later he had soaped it up and had taken Daddy's straight razor to it. Jess had always wanted to shave and although there was still no fuzz showing, he was fourteen years old and it was do or die for him. He had managed to get part of the eyebrow shaved off when mama came into the room and scared him half to death. She had seen him sneak the razor earlier and pretended to be headed outside when she eased back in and popped up behind him. Lucky for Jess, he had just put the razor down and was admiring his handiwork when she went to work on his back side with a hog strap. Daddy, of course, thought it was funny and offered to buy Jess his own shaving kit for Christmas. "You can keep it next to that broken pipe you don't use no more," Daddy said with a chuckle.

That night was also the first chance I'd had to tell everyone about Benny taking us to Troy. I had seen Daddy laugh many times 'til his face turned red, but that night was the first time I had ever seen him (or anyone else, for that matter) fall out of a chair laughing. Daddy said he remembered Benny's arms being all scratched up the next day at the gin, but he knew better than to ask any questions.

Daddy's mood seemed to ease up some this time a year, now that all the cotton had been ginned and shipped off for the season. The extra money Daddy had hoped for with the sharecropping had done well for both sides, and true to their word, the English company Daddy had met with in Mobile continued to buy all the ginned cotton at a premium price. There were some rumors here and there about a pest spreading its way into cotton fields, but that was far away from Coffee County, Alabama, and no one, including Daddy, seemed too concerned about it. He was convinced like most others that the winter chill would kill off the pests before they even reached the state. He had also learned a trick from Daddy Jack that kept most any bug away from a garden, and figured if need be, he could employ the same remedy for the cotton crops. It consisted of boiling cedar-wood shavings, then taking the water and spraying it on the plants. He had been sharing the secret all along with his gin customers and encouraged them to try it on their vegetables for the time being.

Of course, the agricultural agent for the area had been preaching diversification for crops and an increase in the amount of livestock that was raised, just in case the bug paid our area a visit. The problem was there was only so much market for growing vegetables and hogs, and the banks weren't lending much money on any of them. Cotton was king in the South. It was the cash crop and was the only one that could be stored for long periods without spoiling, and then shipped out by train or boat to faraway places.

Cotton was also all the collateral a farmer needed for a bank loan. It had pretty much been that way since Mr. Whitney had come out with his machine over a hundred years ago. Up until that time, all the seeds had to be taken out of the cotton boll by hand and the process just took way too long. I already knew most of this, but what I didn't know I learned in my history class at Troy Normal and had understood for the first time why the South had been so scared of Mr. Lincoln being elected President. The climate and soil were perfect for growing cotton in most Southern states, many a landowner had found it a good way to make a living, and no one down here wanted it messed with by Mr. Lincoln or anyone else.

Of course, there was a war fought over the whole thing and even though there were few shots fired anywhere around Coffee County, when it was over with, we suffered along with Atlanta, New Orleans, and the rest of the South. I remember hearing the old folks talking about how Yankee soldiers were stationed right here in Enterprise, being sent not only to uphold the rights of the free

Negroes but also to protect the hated carpetbaggers and scallywags that swarmed the area. Their ploy was a simple one: take advantage of the already debt-ridden citizens, swindling them out of their land and homes. A running joke in those days was how a farmer came up on an overturned wagon with six carpetbaggers strewn from one side of the road to the other. When a detachment of Union soldiers on patrol came by, they saw the farmer drenched in sweat, throwing dirt into the sixth and final grave. "What happened here?" the captain demanded, recognizing the wagon right off.

"I came up on this mess about an hour ago," the farmer said. "Best I can tell, they must a turned over, and I felt it my duty to bury 'em.

"It killed all six of em?" the captain asked in disbelief.

"Well, three of em said they wadn't kilt yet," the farmer replied, "but ya know ya can't believe nothin a carpetbagger tells ya."

Several years later after the troops left and the local government became friendly again, many land owners found the best way to reclaim much of what the war had cost them was through sharecropping. Of course, their version was much different from what Daddy had now implemented at Melrose. Former slaves and poor white folks entered an agreement to work the fields. The land owner furnished the seed, the tools, and the mules, as well as kept a running tab on everything else they helped to feed or furnish the sharecroppers with. By the time the cotton was harvested, the croppers were usually in such debt they had nowhere else to turn except back to the same life of servitude they had. It was legal slavery, and it usually lasted till the land played out and would hardly grow much more of the white gold the owners were looking for. The croppers would then be asked to leave the property, their land owners not caring where they might go nor how they would provide for themselves or their families.

Now that Sipsey and I were both home from college, Mama let us know about the Christmas party for Melrose School they had planned and what she expected from us. "Everyone is so eager to hear about your new experiences," she said. "We thought it'd be nice if we all sat down to a fine meal, and then you and Sipsey can each tell us all about your new schools and the subjects you've been studyin."

I hadn't thought about it much since I had been gone, but now I remembered how excited everyone was for me and Sipsey the day we departed for college. I had even gotten letters from a few of the students at Melrose and had taken the time to write them back as proper etiquette would suggest. Besides that, I had always gotten excited whenever I had received a post and knew it would affect them the same way it did me. The other thing was, I guess me and Sipsey were now considered by the others "ambassadors for higher education," as one of my professors referred to college students, and several of the cropper parents had vowed to do everything possible to see that their younguns went on to college, too. They saw it as a way out of the ignorance that had held them back all these years, and they wanted their children to be free from it. The grown folks, as far as I was concerned, had nothing to be ashamed of. Their own capacity for learning was amazing. I remember how the consumption of coal oil doubled once they had all learned to read. It wasn't unusual for each family to gather at night, one reading to the rest before going to bed. There was also a ritual twice a week where the men folk would sit drinking coffee and sharing the newspaper. Each article was read and discussed, and even the advertising was talked about at great length. James, who seemed to be the most intrigued by the publication, was invited by Daddy to visit the newspaper office. The publisher was a friend and was always fond of being able to show folks how it worked. Of course, James came back excited to tell everyone the steps it took to print the paper they read.

Neither Sipsey nor I had ever addressed a crowd before, but we both managed to do well enough telling everyone about our colleges and the classes we had taken the first term. When we were done, several folks had questions, and that seemed to relax us and brought to memory several things we had forgotten to say. I also told them about my religion class under Professor Clayton, which made everyone happy about the fact that God had a place at the school and in my education. At the end, I thanked everyone for their prayers and the interest they had.

After we finished, everyone celebrated the gathering with singing and apple cider. Christmas was near. It was in the air and everyone could feel it. The kids were more playful than I had ever seen them and you could tell this year was going to be special. Melrose had managed a bumper crop of cotton because of the good weather and everyone, including the young, knew this had been a blessing. The children shared it with their teacher too, for Mama went home with both arms full of gifts. Some were store-bought, ranging from pieces of fruit Hemp Smith had shipped in, to trinkets and perfume; and then there were a couple of homemade gifts such as a beautiful little carving James had done of a buck and doe deer. I had never seen something made from wood that had so much detail, and before I left that night, I asked him if he could possibly make something for me. He seemed honored to be asked.

Just about the time we pulled up to our house that night, we were greeted with something that rarely happens in our part of the country. Big snowflakes began falling all around us! It had only snowed good one time since I could remember, and I was excited that maybe there would be enough to cover the ground. Jess and me stayed awake half the night looking out the front window hoping it'd never let up, and by morning, our wishes had come true. Daddy woke us up tromping in about daylight from milking the cow, and I overheard him telling Mama that it must be over half a foot in most places. Hearing that, it didn't take long for us to be up and dressed and out throwing snowballs at each other, and when Daddy headed back out to feed the horses, we chased him around the house twice with him screaming bloody murder the whole time. It was still two days till Christmas, but in my mind it had come early. Daddy and Mama both helped us build a snowman and I think they were as proud of it as we were. Mama had read somewhere of how the folks up north made snow angels, and we all took turns leaving our impression of one on a little slope that could be seen from our back porch. With all of the fun and frolic we were having, it seemed that Jess, for once, was going to make it two days straight without getting his back side worked over. He would have made it, too, if ol' Beanard Puckett had been five minutes earlier toting the mail. Jess would have missed him coming and ol' Beanard would have missed being pelted by snowballs.

The next morning was Christmas Eve day. It had always been special to me not only because of the dishes we cooked up, but it was also a time where just Mama and I could talk without the men being underfoot. We had gotten several pies done and set out to cool when Daddy Jack was brought up in conversation.

"I don't begrudge him anymore," Mama said. "About a month ago when Pastor Seth was preachin, I saw a picture in my mind of him. He was smiling at me. I knew from what I saw in that picture that he had always loved me. He just for some reason didn't know how to express it. I had never seen him smile like that before, and it made me feel special. I don't know why I saw that picture that day; there didn't seem to be anything in Pastor Seth's message that brought him to mind, but it came to me, though, and it was real."

I looked at Mama with tears welling up in my eyes. "Mama," I said, "I know why that happened."

I then went on to tell her about the dream I'd had, the story about Daddy Jack's part in the accident that killed Bella, and the picture God had given me that Sunday at communion. The whole time I talked, Mama was nodding her head or covering her mouth as if in disbelief.

"I never knew that whole story," Mama said. "I only knew his sister Bella had died, but no one ever told me all those details. My Lord, thank you God for givin Janie this! The whole thing is beginnin to make sense. Yes, that's exactly why I saw him smilin that day. You forgivin him broke that curse and has released us all, including him."

I saw laughter in her tears after that, the kind where you rejoice over something that can't be put into words. She also shared with me things about Daddy Jack I had never known before. It wasn't bad things; just stories I didn't know. I felt closer to Mama than I had ever felt before.

When Daddy and Jess got back from town, Mama asked me to tell everything over again, which I was glad to do.

"Can you believe that, Winford?" Mama asked. "I never knew God would reach back and forth through time like that to straighten somethin out."

"Well, Jesus did die all those years ago on the cross, and if he can reach forward with his forgiveness like he does, he can certainly reach back a generation or two in our lives and set things right," Daddy said. "Now if y'all are through talkin, can we please eat some pie?"

We had already had a great two days, the kind you wish would last forever, and I had planned to note them in my Big Thank You to God List when we all jumped from a loud knock at our door. It was James.

"Miz Taylor," he said, walking in. "I hope I ain't intrudin."

"Why, no, James, please sit down for some coffee and pie," she said, motioning for me to get it.

Since James was the one who usually spoke up for everyone else, he and Daddy had gotten to be close friends. He knew Daddy was a fair man, and there was trust between them. They had also gotten to hunt and fish together, and Daddy took him to town more frequently than any of the others. Daddy had recently told James as well as everyone else that if they ever wanted to buy land or try their hand at something different, to never feel pent down here at Melrose, but to let him know, and he would help them as much as he could. We all thought this might be what the visit was about until he stood and took something out of his coat pocket.

"I got somethin for Janie and Jess," he said, holding two objects covered with paper and string. "I kinda did it in a hurry for Christmas and didn't wrap it fancy or nothin, but I think they'll like it."

He then reached out and handed us one each. I waited for Jess, knowing he was short on patience. He tore the paper off to find that James had carved for him, from red cedar, an Indian man complete with a war bonnet and holding a bow.

"Just what I wanted!" Jess hollered, jumping up and down.

At school, whenever recess was called, Jess usually had all the others split up into teams of soldiers and Indians and they would play hide-and-capture. Ol' Doolah had given Jess the Indian name of White Wolf years earlier and Jess had never forgotten it.

Then, with everyone looking at me, I unwrapped my gift to find the most beautiful carving of an angel I had ever seen. It was done in white oak. The angel's wings were long and magnificent, her hands were outstretched toward Heaven while she slightly bowed her head in reverence to the One she served. I was astonished — not only by what James had done, but by how fast he had done it.

"How in the world did you make these in less than two days?" I asked him.

"I just picture it in my head and then don't quit 'til I'm done," he answered. "I had an idea on Jess's, but kinda had to guess on what you'd like."

"I couldn't have asked for anything better," I said, hugging him. "It's somethin I will treasure for the rest of my life."

I then talked James into another cup of coffee.

"Nothin takes the chill off a cold night like a good cup of coffee and friendship," I said.

Chapter 13

Working Girl

Like most holidays, mine seemed way too short. It was good to be home with my family though, and that Christmas was the most memorable I had ever had. The snowfall we got and the gift I received from James made it special, but the time and conversations with Mama were things I would treasure forever. Then as if that weren't enough, I found plenty of time to catch up with Sispey, making my whole trip complete. Now a new year and a new term at college were upon us both, and as we headed to Troy and Tuskegee, we again shared our hopes and dreams. They had changed some with all that we had experienced. I was finding life to be that way. The people I had met and things I had learned helped me discover passion for things I had never dreamed of before. We both still had it in mind to be teachers, of course, but Sipsey was now talking about the advantages the North offered to Negroes, especially to someone who would have her kind of education and was capable of sharing it with others. Her going off far away like that was something I didn't want to hear about, but I didn't want to discourage her and figured her mind would change several times by the time we finished college anyway.

She also mentioned working in Tuskegee during the summer and made me promise that if she did, I would come visit her. I had toyed around with finding work myself, not for the summer but after classes during the school term. Aunt Julia had informed me before I left that Byrd's Apothecary was going to be in need of part-time help after Christmas, and knowing I had visited the place regularly last term, she figured I'd be interested. It was the only place in town that had a soda fountain. They also served ice cream during the hot months, and since I wasn't the kind of person to pull a gun and rob an establishment, I figured the best way to get all the money back I had spent there was to go to work for them.

A couple of the classes I took in the new term were ones I knew little about. Biology was required, and we had studied nothing like that at Melrose. The other was theater and stage. The previous term, I had attended several plays that were put on by students, and I thought I'd like to at least try my hand at it. The other subject I went back and forth on until I finally settled on geography. It had been between that and ancient history, and I figured history could wait on me awhile longer. I was trying not to tax my brain too much this time. The fall term had been a shock to me as far as the amount of homework I had to do, and even though I made it through with passing grades, I didn't want to wear myself out again. Besides that, I would be working twenty hours a week at the apothecary and I needed to put my feet up every so often. The one class from the fall I grieved over and would miss this time was Professor Clayton's. Everything I learned from him was something I could lean on for the rest of my life. Now, the only thing I could look forward to was his preaching every Sunday, which was fine, but there could be no hand-raising during his sermons, at least not for questions.

The class I had on Mondays was theater and stage. Our first session was more or less to discuss what we were to be doing the rest of the time. The teacher did have us read from the script of a play called *Our American Cousin*. (I found out later this was the very play Mr. Lincoln had been attending the night he was assassinated.) Of course, I had never play-acted before and although I had the words right in front of me, I stumbled over my tongue time and again, which embarrassed me to no end. I was the first to read, however, and once I saw how the others did, I figured we were pretty much all riding in the same boat. Our teacher, Miss Rachel, assured us this was typical for the first day, and that before we finished the course, we would be full of confidence in our performances and would also know enough about what we were doing to write and direct our own production.

That afternoon was also my first day to work at Byrd's Apothecary. Most of the folks who were employed there recognized me right off from the previous times I had visited, but nonetheless, I was introduced to everyone by Mrs. Byrd and was surprised that most of them knew of my family. One or two even reflected on stories about kinfolk I had barely heard of. One of those who shared something was the owner, Mr. Byrd, who mostly busied himself with mixing medications for the customers. He knew Daddy Jack's brother Russell from long ago and said he remembered the day Uncle Russell had come to Troy to enlist for the army.

"He stopped off by our house to visit and by accident dropped his pocket knife through a crack in the floor while he was peelin a pear. I remember him sayin his grandpa had given him that knife. Seems like before he could fetch it, somethin happened that put his mind in a different direction and he never did retrieve it. Course ya know Russell was killed in that war and I had forgotten all about it myself till about a week ago when we finally tore that ol' house down. I found his knife right where it had laid for over fifty years, no worse for the wear," he said. "As far as I'm concerned, it oughta be yours now."

"Why, I sure would like to have it," I said, "not only for the fact that it belonged to Uncle Russell, but also cause it was my great-great grandfather's too, and I can pass it on to my children, if I ever have any."

"Oh, you'll be married and have young'uns before you know it," Mr. Byrd said, winking at Ms. Byrd. "It happened to us and now we can't get rid of our kids or each other," he said with a hearty laugh.

After Mr. Byrd finished, Miss Ellie, who managed everything else in the store, began going over all my duties, such as how to mix and measure the sodas I would serve. She told me I could also fix myself one soda per day at no cost, but each additional one would be two cents. I managed to make it through the day without much confusion on the formulas, and after several tries I also understood how the register operated.

Mr. Byrd asked if I'd mind dropping off an order for medicine on my way home. Of course, I said I would be happy to. "I kinda hesitate to ask you," he said, "but I figure you'll meet Pink Parker sooner or later anyway."

When I arrived at Mr. Parker's house, the first thing I noticed was a big headstone in his front yard, only a few steps from the street where everyone could easily read the inscription:

ERECTED BY PINK PARKER
TO JOHN WILKES BOOTH
FOR KILLING OLE ABE LINCOLN

I was shocked that anyone would have such a thing in the front yard! Then as I reached the front porch, I heard Mr. Parker rather loudly reciting through an open window a deranged-sounding speech of some sort.

"..and on that day, my friend, when we see once again that glorious flag raised up, yes higher than the Yankee blood that touches the bridles of our horses. And then you and I will mouth the words of that long-forgotten anthem with the ghosts of our fallen brethren from the battlefields of yesteryear. Yes, we will all take up the chorus of *Dixie*, that glorious song that once bellowed across every plantation and cotton field from Texas to South Carolina, and then, my friends, all will know that the South has risen again!" Of course, I was more than happy when Mrs. Parker answered my knock at the door, freeing me from any conversation with her husband.

When I made it to Aunt Julia's, she of course informed me of the great hatred Pink Parker had carried for Mr. Lincoln all these years. "He started that mess in '06," she said. "Oh, you can bet he enjoys all the attention he gets with those reporters comin in from everywhere to do stories. Keeps the North riled up with it and my opinion is, Troy don't need to be known for such a thing. Besides, anyone who would sneak up behind somebody to kill 'em ain't much in my book," she said, rocking forward and spitting the juice from her snuff, "and don't need no monument put up for em, neither."

Years later, I read that when Pink died, his family had the headstone re-inscribed for his burial at Oakwood Cemetery on North Knox Street with no hint of its former tribute.

After sitting awhile, I remembered to show Aunt Julia the pocket knife that had belonged to Uncle Russell. "My lord," she said with tears welling up in her eyes as she reached for it. "He was so proud of this. Grandpa gave it to him about a month before he died himself. Russell must have been about fourteen then, I reckon. I saw him skin many a squirrel and rabbit with this very knife."

"Do you want to keep it?" I asked as she gently rubbed it through her hands.

"No, baby. You keep it and pass it on," she said. "I'm just glad we got it back. I 'spect that tow-headed girl he was courtin must have come by and got his mind off of where he dropped it. Russell met her when he was about twelve and visitin kinfolk here. He was right smitten with her from the start. I remember our brother Leonard told him at breakfast one mornin that it wouldn't do to put sights on her, that she was a close cousin on account of her mama had been married once before to some blood kin of ours. Course the whole thing was a joke, but Leonard had us all go along with it, so Russell left his breakfast settin there and went out to find Mama. By the time he got back, Leonard had eaten his plate of food and Russell's, too, and then he skedaddled, tellin us to inform Russell to go ahead and court that gal, cause the more he thought about it, the more he realized he must be confused over the whole matter," she said, laughing and slapping her knee.

"Yeah, he was determined to muster in here in Pike County so his sweetheart could see him off. I never did hear tell where she got off to once she heard that Russell was dead. That whole war was a widow maker for sure, and those that did make it back were aged way past their years. Paul, who I was married to, used to tell me some of what he saw and went through, and then again, I'm sure there was a lot he held back and wanted to forget about. Course I figured with some a the sleep talkin and hollerin he did, I didn't really want to know past what he told me, anyway.

He did tell bout the time he was captured, though. Told me how he slipped out durin a commotion some of the prisoners was makin. He always laughed when he'd tell that story, cause he had the guards believing his leg was all busted up on the inside and that he couldn't hardly stand, much less walk. When the ruckus started, one of 'em just grabbed his crutch thinkin he wouldn't go nowhere and went off to see what was happenin. Paul said he ran like a jackrabbit for three days till finally he came across some of our Cavalry patrolin. I remember askin him what he ate while he was runnin and he told me all he found was a handful of berries, a few nuts, and some wild onions. Said he had a chance at catchin a rabbit or two, but was too scared to start a fire on account it might have give him away. Ha! Can't you just see the look on that feller's face when he brought that crutch back to Paul and found him gone?" she laughed. "I bet he got a bald spot from all the head scratchin he did tryin to figure out where he got off to."

Then after pausing a minute, Aunt Julia said, "Before he died, he asked me to tailor up his uniform for a regiment reunion they was havin. You should a seen all those old men, so proud and still full of vigor, laughin and cryin over the stories bein told. Then towards the end, they all stood at attention while the roll was called. If someone was missin, the man to his right would give account for him.

"'Killed at Shiloh,' one said.

"'Killed at Blakely,' another answered back. Course it continued on till the last name was called and then the Sargent hollered,

"'Who will carry the flag for these men now they are gone?'

"Then the others, still at attention, all shouted back at once.

"'We will!'

"That was the first and last time Paul got to go to one of those reunions. You know I look back now, and I'm convinced he musta felt like his life was complete, gettin to see all those men he fought beside and trooped with durin the war, cause right after we got back, he just up and died not two weeks later."

After Aunt Julia finished her story, we talked on for quite awhile longer. She seemed to know a little bit about everything, and I enjoyed our conversations no matter what direction they seemed to go. She talked about family and mentioned how I favored my daddy in ways.

"You're always lookin for the humor in situations like he does, but you have a serious side when it calls for gettin things done, and that's just like him, too," she said. "Your daddy don't know it, but it made him right popular around here after he went after those outlaws that day. I overheard people all around town talkin bout what happened on account it made the newspapers here in Troy. One or two folks even said he ought to go on up to Washington and do away with the crooks we have up there; course I'd be scared if he did, cause he'd be too outnumbered." She chuckled. "But I do think you ought to mention it, though. Him runnin for the state senate, I mean. A man with his kind of integrity would represent the people real good, and I think he would carry most the votes in the district. Maybe you could send him a post and get him to thinkin about it."

What Aunt Julia said made perfect sense to me, but I didn't know if it would make any sense to Daddy. He was considered a hero for what he had done, and even though he was one to always wave off the fuss that was made over the incident, he found himself being brought into more and more people's confidence around Coffee County. Judges and merchants alike would go out of their way to confide in him and even the mayor when running for re-election asked Daddy to sit on the podium while he gave his speech. After a little thought, I decided I would take the time to write Daddy such a letter. I also decided I would approach as many people as I could who held some kind of office in Pike County and ask them to sign the letter as well. I figured if Daddy knew there were other folks, besides those at home, ready to stand behind him, he just might take a step of faith.

Chapter 14

Professor Carver

Collecting the signatures was a much easier task than I thought it would be. All of the judges, lawyers, and politicians who served the county would come into the drugstore off and on during the week, and Mr. Byrd introduced me to each one of them. The rumor was that the state senator who represented our district was going to retire when his term was up, and as of yet, no names were circulating to replace him.

Besides all the politicking I had been doing, I found myself knee-deep in study for final exams. I was also preparing for a play several of us were putting together. It was a three-act comedy we titled *Old Salty Dog*. It depicted an aging sea captain who couldn't find it in himself to give up the life he had known since he was a boy. The captain's health had steadily gotten worse over the years; he was hard of hearing and had a stroke, making it almost impossible for his crew to understand the orders he constantly barked out to them. The whole production was a play on words, and once we made the stage with it, we left our audience in stitches. Miss Rachel said that in her entire five years of teaching theater, she had never seen so much thought and effort put into a storyline.

Once the play was finished, I was exhausted. I had started the term thinking I didn't want to overdo myself, but ended up being busy enough for three people. I finally found a full week to do nothing but relax, and I relished every minute of it. There were only two small things left to do, and that was to get a few more signatures for the letter I was preparing for Daddy and to make arrangements for my stay in Tuskegee — both of which I could do at my leisure.

Several times during the school term, Sipsey and I had written letters in anticipation of my upcoming visit, and the last one I received covered many of the details I could expect. The president of her college, Booker T. Washington, had asked Sipsey to house sit for him because he would be spending most of the summer traveling the country raising funds for the next school year. Her duties included keeping the house and yard in order, gathering eggs, picking and putting up vegetables, and most importantly, making sure that Professor Carver, head of their agriculture department, took in at least two nutritious meals per day.

After I arrived in Tuskegee, it became clear to me why such a fuss was made over a grown man eating his food. Professor Carver, one of Tuskegee Institute's most important assets, was prone to spend endless hours working on one project or another, often forgetting to eat — and once classes were over for the summer, his eating habits had only gotten worse. Outside during the day and closed up in his laboratory at night, Professor Carver would lose all awareness of time and ignore the food that was brought to him. After Sipsey threatened to wire President Washington about his eating habits, he finally agreed to start taking all his meals at the house.

"The president doesn't need to be worried about me with all the things he has to be concerned about," Professor Carver said. "Besides, I do find myself needing conversation from time to time, and I couldn't imagine any bigger privilege than to converse with such lovely young ladies."

The first few times I was around Professor Carver, I didn't know what to make of him. He was forty-eight years old, frail looking in build, spoke with a high raspy voice, dressed in a suit that was almost worn out, and made a fuss about placing freshly-cut flowers on the table before our meals. Our first conversations were pleasant enough, but it wasn't until Sipsey had asked me to tell about Benny and our trip to Troy that we all relaxed in each others' company. What started as a chuckle on Professor Carver's part quickly became fits of laughter as he began slapping his leg and holding his stomach while great streams of tears ran down his face. Once we had all settled back down, he stated that if indeed laughter added years to one's life, he knew for sure he would now live well past a hundred. From that evening on, Professor Carver would stay an hour or so past mealtime for conversation, or insist that we gather around the piano to enjoy a few songs with one another.

On one such evening, Professor Carver invited Sipsey and me to his home across campus to share a painting he had just finished and to look at others he had done over the years. Each one was beautiful. The detail and color in all of them were magnificent, and I was astonished to learn that for many of these, he had even made his own paint. Through further conversations with Sipsey about Professor Carver, I could not help but to marvel at the complexity of this man. His gifts seemed to be endless in so many areas, and I found it a mystery as to how he had the time to do it all, including teaching a weekly Bible study, which I had missed the first week but was determined to attend because I was due to leave within the next few days. Once Professor Carver entered the chapel, a hush fell over the room, and each student took out a tablet to take notes. I took no notes myself, but was very touched by his words that evening and found myself remorsefully ashamed by his testimony because of how I had first perceived him.

"You know, God has many ways of speakin to us," he said easing off the front of his desk. "Sometimes it may be through a dream; sometimes you will hear his voice and sometimes there may be a specific verse or story in the Bible he wants you to pay attention to; and of course, there are many other ways as well. I just wanted to share one way in which God spoke to me when I first arrived here at Tuskegee. That was in 1896, and after I had been here only a short while, I became upset and found myself depressed and angry at my circumstances. I had no blood family left on this earth. My father was killed in an accident, and my brother had died some years later from sickness. But even before those tragedies occurred, my mother, sister, and I had been kidnapped by Confederate guerrillas in Missouri when I was but an infant in arms.

"From the story I was told, a man was sent to negotiate our ransom with a racehorse that our owner Mr. Carver had provided. The guerrillas, who intended to sell us all for profit, only gave me back to the negotiator because I was sick to the point of death and not expected to live anyway. We were taken during the winter, and in the bitter cold I developed whooping cough to such a degree that it tore my vocal cords. When I did learn to speak, it was with a high and raspy voice, something that was a bit of an embarrassment to me for many years. As I grew up, I was weak and puny and was only allowed to help with chores around the house for fear I would get sick. During the spring and summer, though, I would take excursions into the woods next to our home, and I would marvel at the trees and plants I saw. I had a hunger to learn all about them. I brought wild flowers and planted them next to our house, savin a few to set the table with.

"As I got older, I was determined to get an education, and I left my home at the age of eight with the blessins of my adopted family. I found work where I could to support myself and pay for the boarding where I stayed. I attended the schools they had established for Negroes at that time, but still had a vast hunger to be educated beyond what was being offered there. The types of things I wanted to learn, you found only at white universities. I applied to one such college and was accepted, only to be turned down when they saw that I was black.

"Then, later and by the grace of God, I was accepted by Simpson College and later by Iowa State Agricultural College, where I graduated. When I finished there, I was offered a lucrative position and a chance to remain among friends, whom I had grown to trust and love over those years. Frankly, I had not felt that secure since I was a little boy living with the Carvers at my home in Missouri. Around this time I began receiving correspondence from President Washington here at Tuskegee. He was asking me to come and be a part of what was being put together.

"I struggled with God for weeks, trying to convince him that I should stay where I was, but in my heart I knew he wanted me here at Tuskegee, where I could do the greatest good for my race.

After I arrived here I became depressed. I saw what little we had to work with: a building that needed to be completed, several shacks, and not one piece of equipment to do experiments with. I was despondent, and after a short while complained to

President Washington, to God, or to anyone else who would listen. I also felt sorry for myself and what I'd had to go through in my life. First, my family was taken from me, then I was often rejected because of my race, and now to top it all off, my close friends seemed a thousand miles away. I felt I had made a mistake by coming here and thought I might have even misunderstood what God had impressed on me when I had prayed for a decision about the matter.

"One morning after I had put all my thoughts together and brought them before God, I found myself doubtful that he would answer me because of the attitudes I had taken. But then as I was about to finish my time with him that morning and just as the sun was rising, I asked him straight out, 'God, is this where you want me?' and the moment I did, I felt the urge to look up, and there, sitting not more than ten feet from me, was the most beautiful white dove I had ever seen. I immediately knew that *yes*, I was supposed to be here, and that God was also here with me in my endeavors. I was humbled that he had answered my prayer so quickly and in spite of my childish attitudes. I have been at this institute now for almost eighteen years, with the only thing lacking in my life being a good fit of laughter, and by the grace of God, He has even now provided this through a new-found friend," he said, smiling at me.

"Anyway, I shared these things with all of you because perhaps at times, you might have doubts of your own. If this is the case, I encourage you to bring them all before God as I did and still do. Don't be afraid to ask Him questions when you meet with Him. He loves you every bit as much as He loves me or anyone else.

"Now, I am about through," he said walking over to close a window. "but I did want to leave you with a couple of helpful things to remember when seeking to meet with God. One is to rise early and find a place of solitude. Wake before the world does and the day gets busy and starts pulling on you. The second thing is to meet with Him in a spirit of fasting. In other words, besides a little water, do not eat or drink anything before you start your prayer time. By doing this, you will be setting your body aside so that your spiritual senses will be keen, and you can sit quietly and listen. Of course, start off in prayer, and while doing so, follow the example Jesus gave his disciples to follow, elaborating on those areas he mentioned. Finally, I tell you not to get discouraged. It will take practice, but the more you meet with Him, the better you will begin to hear and understand what he is saying to you; and remember this above all else: Our Creator God always gets goose bumps when he sees his children coming to meet with him."

After he had finished speaking and all were dismissed, Sipsey and I invited Professor Carver to visit with us and to try out some of the blueberry pie Sipsey had left to cool while we were at Bible study. Professor Carver was delighted by our invitation.

"I kinda thought I might be wearing out my welcome," he said with a bright smile, "but you know I have to walk by there anyway, and if I had not been invited and smelt that pie, I think I would have had to go back before God with more complaining," he said with a laugh.

Once we each had our fill, Sipsey insisted on doing the dishes, and Professor Carver and I went out to the porch, which gave me a chance to express my feelings on what he had said earlier. "Professor Carver," I started, "I wanted you to know how very, very sorry I am for what you have had to go through in this life. It seems as though you have already suffered enough tribulation for three people while you have been here on this earth. I also wanted to confess that when I first met you, I looked upon you as being weak because of your small stature and voice. Then when I heard your story, it made me ashamed that I had judged you that way," I said. "Now I am wondering if you could ever find it in your heart to forgive me, because I would like very much to be counted among your friends."

Of course, by the time I had finished my confession, my bottom lip was quivering and big tears were finding their way down my cheeks.

"My dear child," he said, patting me on the arm, "do not give the matter another thought. It would be a privilege to be your friend, and as far as what I have been dealt in life, I consider that a privilege also, knowing what my Savior had to endure on my behalf. Besides, I have found that when God puts things, even tragedies, in your life to change the road you are traveling on, it is because he wants to bless you and he knows in his infinite wisdom that it would not have been possible to do so if you had stayed in your present circumstances."

The next evening found the two of us visiting once again. Sipsey had to make choir practice that night and with her not being around, I was much less likely to carry on foolishness and could speak on more serious matters. Professor Carver started the conversation by asking about my life and ambitions and in so doing, I had mentioned how I came to meet Sipsey as well as the school my mother had started for the sharecroppers' children. I could tell he was touched by what my family had done for them and their parents, but I was quick to point out that we were the ones who were truly being blessed. Then after telling him about operations at the cotton gin, I could see that Professor Carver was about to say something, but then he paused as if he needed to choose what his words should be.

"It might not be my place to tell you this, Janie," he said, "but I'm afraid of what is about to happen to your father's ginning business. I'm also afraid for the cotton crops that are being grown on y'all's plantation. See, there's an insect that crossed over from Mexico some years back and has now made its way through Texas and Louisiana. Some folks thought it would be stopped by the Mississippi River because of the river's great width, but there are reports that it has already started infesting the cotton in Mississippi as well. There have been several attempts to stop the spread of the pest with sprays and poisons, but all efforts have been futile thus far. You might or might not have heard your father mention this," Professor Carver said. "Its common name is the boll weevil."

"Yes, sir," I replied, nodding my head, "I have heard him mention it more than once to the folks he buys cotton from. I don't think he realizes how far it has spread, though, because the last time it was brought up at our table, he thought that it was just in Texas and Louisiana. He also thought a good freeze or two would kill the boll weevils off before they became a nuisance around here, but from what you have just said, it looks as if they are determined to survive no matter what concoction is put on them or what the climate is," I said with worry in my voice.

"Well, as you know, I run the agriculture department here at Tuskegee," Professor Carver said, "and that's what I get paid for. But every opportunity I have, I will travel out to the farms in the area and share any new information I learn from my experiments. One thing I try to impress on the farmers when I do this is the importance of rotating their crops. Cotton, the one that is so important to so many, depletes the soil of its nitrogen and that's why all the families your father was so gracious to take in were kicked off the land in Huntsville. Now, if that farmer up there had had them plant something like cow peas for just one season, it would have replenished the soil a good bit, and he would have been astonished at what his fields would have made in cotton the following year. He could have then rotated his fields using half of his land for certain types of food crops and the other acreage for cotton, and I guarantee you he would have put more money in the bank than any of his neighbors who grew only cotton.

Well anyway, it now looks as if what I have been preaching to the farmers around here about these methods is bound to come about. I just hate that folks will be forced to plant the crops I suggested to them on all their land for no-telling how long, because as you know, our economy is not really set up for anything but cotton, and there is no large market in Dixieland for anything else," he said, sounding exasperated. Then while rising from his chair to leave, Professor Carver predicted, "I think south and central Alabama as well as parts of Georgia will get one, maybe two more cotton yields before we are invaded by the pest."

The next morning as Sipsey and I were gathering eggs, Professor Carver called for me while standing some distance away.

"I want to show you something before you leave, Janie, if you don't mind getting a little dirty," he said as I came up closer.

We then made our way through a little patch of woods until we arrived in a field of some of the healthiest cotton I had ever seen.

"It's still got a ways to go before it blooms, but the reason it's so healthy lookin is because these fields were planted in cow peas and sweet potatoes the last three years. My intention is to use this acreage to impress the local farmers about the importance of replenishing the soil. Somehow now, though, I feel as if God is wanting me to accomplish more than can be done with peas and potatoes," he said, "and I have been thinking on what that could be; but I haven't been able to discern exactly what God's intentions are, so I guess for the time being I will have to wait and trust him until I see his full purpose unfold. It's truly beautiful when that happens, you know, when God's plans all come about – I mean, it's like a flower that finally opens, and you get to see its beauty for the first time." He then illustrated, by slowly opening his hand. "I will tell you this much, though. I am convinced that what God is trying to show me has something to do with a plant I have already done a good bit of research on. For just yesterday morning, while I was talking to God about how I could best help the farmer, he simply asked, 'Have you considered the peanut?' Now, I have already spent quite some time and effort in impressing on people the importance of this plant. Especially for those who are lacking protein in their diets, but so far, it has never seemed to be a crop anyone is interested in growing."

Then pulling out a handful of peanuts from his pocket, he said, "There's been a stigma about this little legume for years. Folks didn't think they were good for human consumption; so they fed them only to their livestock. Even now, though people understand the peanut's nutritional benefits much better, they still won't grow but a patch or two of them. But last night in a dream, I saw myself standing in a field full of these." He held out his hand showing me. "Folks rushing up from all over and begging me to share them. When I woke up, I could only laugh about what I had dreamt, for like I've already stated, no one ever seemed to be that interested in the peanut's usefulness," he said tossing a few in his mouth. "But I am convinced it is further confirmation of what God wants me to do; I just think my timing has to be right when I take this same advice back to the farmers again, and I hope maybe this time the white farmers will listen, too."

After seeing firsthand what rotating crops could do for cotton production, I was excited for the chance to share the information with Daddy. We all knew our next crop should be plentiful because of the snow we had gotten in December. There was an old saying handed down for generations among plantation owners—"The more the snow, the more cotton we grow"—and it usually proved to be true as long as there weren't too many hard rains or hailstorms once the plant reached a certain point of growth. What could be done year after year with these methods of crop rotation was something that every cotton grower in the South should practice, and at Melrose, where we had fields not being used for anything, the whole idea would work especially well. There was, however, something that worried me: the boll weevil infestation Professor Carver had talked about the night before. If the pest did make its way to our part of the country, it wouldn't matter how much we practiced the new methods I had just seen; there wouldn't be any cotton to harvest, no matter how healthy the soil became for growing it.

During my train ride home, I thought about the ramifications of this possible invasion and if anything, my fears just got bigger. Our livelihood depended on cotton—not so much from what we grew, but from the ginning business Daddy owned. It's how we made our money, paid our bills, and bought the things we could not grow. It's also how my education, as well as Sipsey's and that of many others, was being paid for at the colleges and universities across the South. I also thought about it from the croppers' point of view: They had already been kicked off one plantation, and although I knew Daddy wasn't about to do the same sort of thing to them, there were several who had saved up to a point of where if they wanted to, they could put a down payment on land of their own. Of course, it would take cotton to make it all work, and even if they stayed at the plantation, the money they had put back would eventually be used up on the sort of things we all need just to get by on. Also, there was the hope a few of them had mentioned about getting their own children off to college, but if Mr. Boll Weevil made his presence known in our part of the country, the croppers could forget that dream.

The whole thing put my mind in a quandary, and for the first time in my life I knew what it felt like to be depressed over something. Up until now, the worst thing I had worried about was making sure my grades were good at school, and that was nothing compared to what I was fretting about now. As I stepped off the train in Enterprise, I realized for my own well being that I'd have to take the same attitude I had heard others take, and that was to "just cross that bridge when you get there."

Chapter 15

All about Cotton

Daddy had not been informed of exactly what day or hour I would be arriving back in town, but I knew as long as I pulled in by four o'clock, I could easily catch him at the cotton gin. After I walked the short distance from the depot to the gin, he spotted me toting my luggage and came quick-stepping out to greet me.

"Well, I will just be," he said, grabbing me up in a big hug. "I didn't know my baby girl was due in today. Did your mama even know you was gonna be here?"

"No, sir. I just thought I'd surprise all a y'all without causin too big a fuss this time," I said, smiling.

"Give me just a half hour to finish up here and then we'll be on our way," he said, pointing with aggravation at some of the machinery.

On our trip home, I had Daddy's full attention about my just-completed college term and filled him in on everything from my job, to Uncle Russell's knife being found, to my trip to Tuskegee and the crop-rotating experiments Professor Carver had done.

"So you say he's got a real healthy crop growin after plantin cow peas and sweet potatoes in those fields?" he asked, sounding rather surprised.

"Yes, and Daddy, you should have seen how thick and tall it was standin! I don't even think our first crop was as good as what I saw in those fields," I replied, "and I want to tell ya, white or black, I have never met anyone like Professor Carver. He is so knowledgeable about so many things, includin which process to use on which crop so as to get the most out of it. He told me cotton is a plant that pulls a lot of nitrogen from the ground. If it's grown over and over in the same fields, it will eventually deplete the soil to the point where you won't get anything but bumble-bee cotton," I said as daddy nodded his head in agreement. "I brought you several pamphlets that he gave me, and he said if you could ever spare the time, he would be honored to meet you at the college and show you several of the things they have been workin on."

"I'd love to, Janie," Daddy said, "but with my duties at the gin, it would be a spell before I could take the time off. 'Sides, if you saw what he did was successful, we'll give it a try come next plantin season ourselves; we were gonna have to cut our cotton in half anyway."

Daddy then went on to inform me that three of the cropper families had recently moved on. The way he told it, one of them had been contacted by a cousin in Conecuh County about a plantation that was about to get foreclosed on. After some correspondence with the bank in Evergreen, it was agreed the land could be sold in quarters, with each family, including the cousin, winding up with just over two hundred acres each. Of course, Daddy held no ill will about any of it, and even gave them cotton seed and other goods to help them get started.

I guess we all knew this day would come sooner or later. Folks had a right to better themselves, and we knew our family had done only a small part by offering them an opportunity. It was up to them to take advantage of it, and so far, every one of them has done that. They had all worked hard in the garden and fields, covering most of their own food needs and making money off the cotton they'd grown. They also took the time to learn and better themselves with an education. It was something they'd probably have no second chance at, and they grabbed hold of it with both hands while they could.

As far as the Melrose School went, I also knew Mama was tired and ready to quit teaching. She had told me on my last visit home that it was getting tougher and tougher to satisfy everyone with new school work, and now that the younger kids had been there almost seven years, any one of them would be welcome to a job that required writing and arithmetic. Yes, things were changing for sure, and nothing proved that more than the extra foot of growth I saw on Jess the moment we pulled up to Melrose. He was tall and slim and lookin more and more like Daddy. I also noticed his voice was changing and thought I saw just a hint of fuzz showing above his upper lip. The first chance he got, he started complaining about all the chores he was responsible for since I had been off to college, but he quieted down once I bragged on how much the wood cutting had seemed to fill him out.

After slipping quietly inside the house and finding Mama busy in the kitchen, I eased up to the table behind her, then real quiet-like, pulled out a chair and sat down. It was all I could do not to laugh, especially when she went to talking to herself about what food she had just messed up for supper.

"They'll just have to be happy with what I've got cooked," she said, "cause I'm just one person, and I can't run around all over creation all day and then come home and make a perfect supper every night."

Then without paying me a bit of attention, she walked right past me to the front door and hollered for Daddy and Jess to come to the table. It was on her way back to the kitchen that she finally noticed I was sitting there, and she screamed bloody murder. I laughed 'til I nearly fell off the chair, and once Mama was over her shock at the sight of me coming home unannounced and sneaking up on her, she joined in as well. Daddy and Jess came running as soon as they heard Mama scream, but finding out the commotion was over nothing more than her being surprised, they both just stood there shaking their heads, looking like a set of twins.

I knew when I had left for school after the Christmas break, the relationship I shared with my mother had forever changed, and although we still teased and picked at one another, our conversations were now centered on more serious matters. Unlike Daddy, she had accepted the fact I was almost grown, and she treated me more as an equal when it came to sharing information and asking my opinion about things. Daddy meant no harm and at times he seemed to be caught somewhere in the middle when it came to my becoming a woman. He had always doted on me as his little girl, and although I enjoyed the attention I received, I also wanted to be taken seriously when I had something important to say. The information I had given him about Professor Carver's cotton experiment was one thing he took to heart and even asked me to share with Mama what I had seen in Tuskegee on my visit there. Once supper was finished everyone but Jess, who had to finish his chores, moved into the parlor. There, daddy took straight to his chair and reached for his pipe makings. Once he got it packed in and lit good, he began reading the pamphlets I had given him earlier that day.

"My gosh, this Professor Carver even talks about why cotton produces more when there has been snow durin the year. Accordin to him, it puts nitrogen in the ground just like certain food crops do, just to a lesser degree. I guess what we can do is plant some of those crops on the acreage we was gonna rest, bein that our other folks are gone now. We won't need to tend 'em much, and when it's time, we'll just plow the crops under so as to put them nutrients in the soil like he's talkin bout here. Then we'll swap up where we plant the cotton to those fields the next go-round and see what we get."

I was happy that Daddy was more than amused at the information Professor Carver had taken the time to send him. I also knew we had a problem coming our way with the boll weevil, something that was sure to worry Daddy a good bit. Like most men, he was one to fret over things, and it was worse when the problem was out of his control and he couldn't fix it himself. Knowing this, I was a little nervous to even bring the subject up, but felt it was my duty to pass along the information I'd learned. After I shared with Daddy what Professor Carver had told me, I was surprised and relieved at what Daddy already knew about the situation.

"Yeah, one of them fellers from England who buys cotton from us came by last month and told me all about it," Daddy said nodding his head. "It don't look good at all. Said they've been forced to start buyin from other countries already just to meet the demands they have. 'Course, they'll keep buyin from us as long as we can send 'em the stuff. Also, his prediction on the situation was just like your friend Professor Carver's was – one, maybe two more good crops before we get infested. I just feel sorry for all those growers in Texas, Louisiana, and now Mississippi. They've lost their source of income for who knows how long, and then you also got those who had a bank note for one reason or another.

They'll end up losin their homes and land if they haven't already. The whole thing is just sad," he said, easing up in his chair. "and it's gonna get worse before it gets any better. I use to hear my daddy say, 'It ain't good to run all your rabbits into one hole. I never knew exactly what he meant when he'd say that, but I do now. The good thing for us is we own this land and all we really have to fret about is the taxes; as far as what we eat, we already grow a right smart of it anyway, and when it comes down to it we can share that with our neighbors if we find any of 'em short on something."

Then after pausing for a moment to re-light his pipe, he continued, "You know, it seems like the South never did learn its lesson. It's always been about cotton down here. In a way, if you stop to think about it, that little white fuzzy ball is what caused that war everybody still talks about. You think about it. If'n it hadn't become so popular, the folks who lived back then wouldn't have needed all those slaves to work the fields, and I don't think there never would have been a hand raised, North or South. And then, as far as makin a livin goes, I'm sure we could a come up with somethin to do without havin to buy another soul to do all the work. 'Course I'm one to talk. I'm in the ginnin business and that machine is what made the whole situation so profitable to begin with. I guess what I'm a getting at is, we been put in our place once before over our way of life, and what we've always counted on so much and now, even though there won't be troops comin from the North this time, our enemy is gonna march right through Dixie—and cotton'll still be the reason why."

I could tell from Daddy's tone that he was through talking for the night, and I felt it'd be better to not bring up the idea Aunt Julia had given me about his running for a state office. Besides, I hadn't even taken the time to share with Mama yet what I had been putting together, and I sure wanted her blessings before I said a word to Daddy.

After several minutes of silence passed, Jess came stomping in through the front door, complaining about having to feed the horses, something he was supposed to have done earlier in the day.

"I'll tell you what! I think I'm just gonna run away from home for a while and let somebody else worry with all these chores. Seems like I'm the only one around here who does anything, and I'm getting plum tired of it!" he railed, waiting in vain for someone to sympathize with his plight.

"Well then, just go ahead, boy!" Daddy hollered back, while uncrossing his legs and sitting up real quick like. "That'd be one less mouth to feed around here, and I won't have to worry about things bein done right, either! Besides, I'm tired a arguin with ya! You been gettin too big fer yore britches these last few months, and I'm here to tell ya, as far as life goes, you don't know diddly squat!" He said slapping the arm of his chair.

Jess had no idea that Daddy would call his bluff so quickly, and feeling like he had to own up to his words, he slowly backed out the same door, all the while telling us how sorry we'd be in a day or so when the work piled up. Once he was gone, it took all we could do not to bust out laughing. Jess had been complaining ever since I left for college, and now that Daddy had to leave early for work each morning, Jess shouldered more responsibilities. Of course, every one of Jess's tasks was somethin that could be done by the rest of us in a couple of hours; but he was stubborn in his thoughts and liked to exaggerate his misfortunes. After the lights were turned down, Mama and I peeped out the window, hoping we could catch a glimpse of Jess somewhere in the shadows.

"He'll probably sleep in the barn if he don't get too scared," Daddy chuckled, "but I betcha by mornin he'll be right out there on the front porch curled up behind those chairs so nothin won't get 'im."

And Daddy was right. When Jess figured we must all be asleep, I heard him creeping up onto the porch and lying down just where Daddy said he would be. Then the next morning as we sat eating breakfast, Jess came traipsing in through the back door. I knew the smell of bacon was more than he could resist, and to top it off, the three of us all just sat there carrying on about how well we had rested the night before and how good the new jam was that Mama had just opened. We were all watching Jess out of the corner of our eye to see how long his pride would hold up and what his first words might be. After Jess stood there being ignored for several minutes, our kitten came up purring and begging for his attention. Jess, now seeing his chance to break the silence and ease the embarrassment he had caused himself, squatted down and began rubbing him with long tender strokes, finally saying, "Well, I see y'all still got the same ol' cat!"

We all bellowed out with laughter and knew right off that what we had just heard would be repeated frequently by the three of us and by the future generations of our family, all of which chawed Jess to no end.

Later that morning and once Daddy had left, I did get to speak with Mama about the conversation I'd had with Aunt Julia.

"Oh, I think it's a real good idea," Mama said, "and there have already been several folks includin Judge Sweat mention this very thing to your daddy. Now, he doesn't think he's up to public office, but I told him that's exactly what people want these days, someone who's not tryin to make their whole life's livin out a politics. He also said that even though he's known around here, there are parts of the district where he knows barely a soul, like over in Pike County. 'Course now, with that letter you brought home he won't get to use that as an excuse, and if we get infested by the boll weevil like he says we will, he'd better have some way of keepin busy, cause I'm not about to have both him and Jess under my feet every day!" she said, barely laughing.

The rest of the day Mama and I spent talking over details. The election for state senators was not that far away, and we knew if Daddy was to have a chance, we would need to get busy. Mama suggested I write the folks who had signed my letter in Troy, those who had expressed an interest in backing daddy for office, and let them know his hat would be in the ring. She also suggested that as soon as I returned to college, I should apply for my last semester internship to be done right here at Melrose School. Her thoughts were that if Daddy did agree to run for the office and won, he would want her in Montgomery with him during orientation procedures. By the end of the day, we had worked out all the details, and in our minds, we already had Daddy elected. The only thing left to do was to make him think that the whole idea had been mostly his.

Chapter 16

Running for Office

From that day through the rest of the summer, I found myself busier than I would have ever imagined. As God would have it, while Mama and I were putting all of our plans together, Judge Sweat and the sitting state senator Robert F. Hamlin were that very day paying Daddy a visit at the cotton gin. Seems that Daddy had made the statement to Judge Sweat that if Senator Hamlin would back him as a candidate for the office he was retiring from, then he might seriously consider the notion to run for his seat. Daddy confessed that he had no idea if any of what he had promised would ever pan out and hadn't given it much thought since the day they had the conversation. After arriving home and first being excited about the opportunity, he then began sounding doubtful, as if he wasn't quite sure about what he was getting himself into.

"Well, I guess as soon as I can trust James to handle the ginnin business, I'll try my hand at somethin I know nothin about, and to top it off, the first bit of advice Senator Hamlin has given me is I should make my way over to Troy when I have a chance and introduce myself to a whole bunch a folks who have never even heard my name before," he groused, sounding as if he'd rather yank a tooth out.

"Well, Daddy, I reckon me and God are about two steps ahead of you," I said, "'cause most of the folks you're worried about meetin have done heard the name Winford Taylor. They became familiar with it the first time it made the papers over there, after you led that posse to those outlaws, and then most of those who now hold some kinda office over there heard it not more than a month or so ago when I approached them on your behalf."

I then handed Daddy the letter. He sat there in silence, reading it word for word and looking over all the signatures I had collected.

"I don't know why," Daddy said solemnly, "but I am convinced God has gone before me on this whole thing, and I'm in no position to question Him on the matter. I know lots of things He does don't make any sense 'til later on and sometimes you may even have to make Heaven before you understand it at all. But with y'all's help, I'll just do the best I can runnin for this senate seat, and then, if I am fortunate enough to win the thing, I'll do my best to serve the ones who entrusted it to me—but before I even start on any of that, I'd like to have some supper. It won't do, me getting so skinny that folks can't see who their a votin for."

Now that Daddy had committed to be a candidate, Mama and I wrote letters to all the folks I had previously met in Troy and to every office holder and newspaper in our district. As far as the newspapers were concerned, it was our idea to remind the prospective voters through their written pages just who Dison Winford Taylor was: the man who had been responsible for the swift justice of three murdering outlaws. We also contacted individuals whom Senator Hamlin said could be trusted to make donations without expecting personal favors in return. Finally, by the end of the summer and right before I went back to college, we had more than half the money we had hoped for safely deposited in the bank and the rest of it pledged to come in whenever it was called for. We knew there would be lots of expenses incurred from travel and advertisements, and wanted to make sure they were all covered without hurting our own finances.

The day I was to leave for school, I made the trip into town with Daddy by buggy. He kept the horse at a slow walk, which gave us a chance to enjoy the sun rise, and time to catch up on things we had missed talkin about during the summer.

"Yeah, ya know ol' Benny's mama Miss Emma, who runs that boardin house?" he asked while I nodded my head. "Well, last month she had a couple stayin there who was just passin through, and one mornin the lady comes out tellin everybody she's worried cause she can't get her husband to wake up. Miss Emma wat'n there, so Benny took off by himself to check on the man and come back a minute or so later and starts pattin the lady on her shoulder."

"I'm sorry, ma'am," Benny told her, "but there ain't nothin we can do for your husband now; he's done stiff as a board."

Of course I hated it for the lady who had lost her husband, but as far as how Benny handled the situation I could only shake my head and laugh.

Then Daddy went on to tell me about Sipsey's brother Spookie. He had gotten to sneaking around and stealing all the little white sugar cookies the croppers' wives had made for their three o'clock get together. It was a British custom one of the ladies had read about in some book and thought it was a good practice for them to adopt, although they drank coffee instead of tea. The men teased them unmercifully about it, but flat-out denied having anything to do with taking the cookies or having any knowledge of their theft. Then, after the third time, the women had had enough. They threatened to stop preparing meals for the men until a confession was made or the thief caught. Knowing there had to be an end to it, or starve to death, James volunteered to hide out in the rail car after dark so he could catch whoever was stealing the ladies' happiness. Figuring it must be one of the children, James put the grown folks up to telling ghost stories around the fire that night. Then after everyone retired for the evening, he himself eased up into a corner of the car and covered himself with an old bed sheet. It was a full moon that night and after sitting for what he figured to be two hours, he finally heard steps coming up the ramp and into the car. Looking through the two eye holes he had cut, James could see plain as day that the culprit was Spookie, who ate two or three of the cookies where he stood and then proceeded to put the others in the pockets of his coveralls. Without being seen, James eased up and moved several feet behind Spookie, all the while making little ghost-like sounds as he went. Spookie, hearing the noise, slowly turned to see a restless spirit swaying back and forth.

Later, when I heard the story from James, he said he had never seen anyone's eyes bug out so far, as if they were on stems! He also said he had never seen anyone move that fast once Spookie's feet got to going. "He ran into the wall the first time," James said, "but made the door on his second try, and when he did, he weren't stoppin for nothin or nobody. Then," James said, hardly able to talk for laughing, "when we all set down for breakfast the next mornin, my wife Isabel puts Spookie's plate down with nothin on it but four a them little sugar cookies. He just sat there awhile starin at 'em until we all went to makin little ghost sounds and gigglin. He then stood up and walked away, lesson learned."

As much as I enjoyed being home for the summer, it wasn't until I had returned to Troy that I truly felt rested. I started back to work at Byrd's the day after I arrived and picked right up where I had left off in June. Mr. and Mrs. Byrd seemed delighted that I was back at their establishment and filled me in on several things I had missed out on since I had been gone.

"We have a new visitor from time to time around the back of the building," Mrs. Byrd said. "We call him Pippin 'cause that's the only name he gave us to go by. You'll see him occasionally when you're throwin things out for the burn pile. He'll get it goin and tend it for awhile so we won't have to. When he does, just grab a quarter from the register and fix 'im up a soda and he'll be obliged. By the way, he's not very talkative, so don't let it hurt your feelins if he's short on conversation with ya."

After several days, I did have a chance to meet him myself. "You must be Pippin," I said, carrying an armful of boxes. "I'm Janie and have just gotten back after bein home for the summer."

Mrs. Byrd was right, for he returned nothing back as introduction, other than a slight nod of his head. I then fetched his quarter and soda and handed it to him, not expecting any thanks or conversation.

"Where's home at fer ye? If you don't mind me askin," Pippin asked shyly.

"Oh, not at all," I answered back. "It's a few miles outside of Enterprise on a plantation we call Melrose – a place we inherited from my mama's daddy when he passed away several years ago."

Then realizing that what I had just said might have come across as bragging, I quickly changed the subject.

"I don't know if you have time to fool with it or not," I said, "but my Aunt Julia who lives several blocks from here wanted me to ask around for someone to help her get a little catch-all building made. She already has a good stack of lumber and says it's time to get it done, cause she's tired a trippin over things and is willin to pay good money if someone can get it built."

"Tell her you found the man," Pippin said eagerly. "I can start on it tomorrow if that ain't too soon."

Then after giving him directions to Aunt Julia's, I excused myself so I could finish up things in the store.

The next day was Saturday, and Pippin showed up shortly after daylight. "I didn't know who might be here to hold up a board for me, so I brung my oldest boy to help me out," Pippin said.

Then after Aunt Julia showed him what she wanted done, they started cutting and laying out all the lumber according to size. By lunchtime, I saw that Pippin and his son were well on their way to being done. I called them up to the house to eat.

"Looks like y'all done this kinda thing before," I said, smiling at Pippin's son, who had come up onto to the porch first.

"Yes, ma'am. We built our own house in Mississippi," the boy said, trying to sound grown up, "and we'd still be livin there if it wadn't for that bank takin it back from us. Took our land and house both, not long after that bug ate all our cotton."

What the boy said was loud enough for everyone to hear, including his daddy, who was just now coming up the steps.

"Aaron," Pippin cautioned the boy as his own face blushed with embarrassment, "these folks don't want to hear our hard luck stories."

After we all finished eating, Pippin and Aaron excused themselves from the table to finish up what they had started, which didn't take them long. Once they were done, Aunt Julia was quite pleased with their work, so she paid a bit more than Pippin must have expected.

"Well, ma'am, I didn't hardly think our labor was worth that much," he said. "You also fed us and topped it off with some a them apple tarts, which is the best I ever et."

"I can tell good work when I see it," Aunt Julia said with a smile, "and I got other things need to be done round here if you're willin to come back in a couple of weeks. And bring your boy again, too, cause it might take more than just you to get it done."

That night, I was more than curious and determined to find out what Pippin's story was. I could tell from what his son had said that they had come on some hard times. I also knew Pippin was eager to do whatever he could to take care of his family without coming across as a beggar. After thinking about it a while, I figured the best way to get him to open up was maybe to talk about things we might have in common, such as what I'd picked up from Aaron about losing their cotton crop to the boll weevil. A couple of days later behind Byrd's, I had the chance to do just that.

"You know what I was tellin you the other day bout that plantation we live on?" I asked Pippin as he nodded. "Well, my daddy was sayin how he was worried about those bugs from Mississippi that're headed our way. We know it's just a matter of time fore they make it here and we're dreadin it for two reasons. One's on account of the cotton that's grown on our land and the other's cause of the cotton gin my daddy owns. We know our chances for cash money are gonna be wiped out when those bugs get here, and Daddy said he can't see any chance of them bein stopped, either."

"Those lil ol' bugs shore got us," Pippin said despairingly, while poking at the fire. "Took just about ever thang we owned. What little was left, we sold for food and train tickets and managed to get right here to Troy, still a mite short a South Carolina though, where we was hopin to end up. I got a brother who lives up there and he's been a sharecroppin for a feller. Say's this man has a good market growin and shippin out goobers, somethin I never seen a whole lotta use for, but my brother says this man can be trusted, so I figured with things bein the way they are, we'd try and get there soon as we could. Course they done got this year's crops planted and I don't reckon they'd be willin to share much of the profits, seein how I wadn't there to start with the plantin. As far as that bug you was talkin about, we did manage to get a little of our cotton in the first season and was sure we'd be safe on the next one, figurin they had all died durin the winter or gone off back to hell where they was from. But I guess they just burrowed down and waited like some kinda demon lookin for a washed and spotless soul, cause when they came back on the next crop we was seven times worse off."

Then, shaking his head, Pippin said, "I'm sorry to use that kinda language in front a you, Miss. It's just that we put ever cent we had into that land and building onto our little house and barn. It was sure nice thinkin for the first time in my life I had somethin. Somethin I could even pass on to my sons when I got older, kinda like yore grandpaw done for y'all. Course you heard Aaron say how the bank got it all back from us. After that happened there, wadn't no reason to stay; so me, my wife Bonnie Kate, and our boys headed out. Been here bout two months now just doin odd jobs here and there. I struck a deal with Mr. Barbaree out close to Jonesville not long after we got here. He needed some work done on his house and feed cribs, so I traded with him for a dry place to sleep in the loft of his barn. Course, he lets us pick from his garden and visit the smoke house, too, so we ain't starvin. Still, I find myself plum rattled bout what to do." Then pausing and choking back tears, said. "I feel like we ought to be movin on, but I ain't got the money to get very far and don't know what kinda situation it'd put us in if we did." He then quickly caught hold of his emotions, gave me a short nod and walked away.

That night as I reflected on what Pippin had said, I realized how folks considered their circumstances. It's one thing to hear or read about tragedies or troubles when they are hundreds or thousands of miles away, like that big ship the *Titanic* that had sunk in the Atlantic Ocean about a year ago. But it never strikes your heart until you meet someone who was actually in a hard situation, and when they give you an account of it firsthand, that's when you can see it in their eyes, for those reflect a deep, dark nothingness that says they have nothing to look forward to. It was through my conversation with Pippin that I understood how bad things really were, both for those who had already lost what they'd had because of the pest and for all of those who were in its path.

Of course, Pippin and his family still had their lives, and it's always worse when you lose the folks you love, but any of it can be bad, especially when you have no one to turn to and you're

convinced that God has raised his hand to cause the situation to
start with—or worse yet, that He just sat by and did nothing to stop
it. I saw that in Pippin's eyes and heard it in his voice, and all I
knew to do for him was pray. I knew I needed to pray for others as
well, for those who had already been hit by the boll-weevil plague
and for those who were about to suffer it. I did a little bit of
praying that night, but decided not to be lax in the amount of time I
devoted, nor feel as if I was plowing around the stump when it
came to asking God for his help. So I woke at four o'clock the next
morning, knowing I would be rested, and could pay more attention
to what I needed to say.

It was two weeks later when I saw Pippin again. School had
started for me and took up most of my mornings, which was when
he usually came by the apothecary. But he did remember the work
Aunt Julia had promised him, and he showed up on a Saturday
with Aaron to get it started. He didn't know it, of course, but I had
written Daddy on Pippin's behalf and had received a post back
from him on the matter just the day before. I knew I had to be
careful with how I approached Pippin about going to Melrose, and
I felt if I said it just right, he would understand it to mean his
services were needed and that there would be no handout in the
deal. By the time he and Aaron broke for lunch, I had pretty much
figured out the best way to put it to him. After I finished, Pippin
seemed to be excited with the prospect of having a place to live
and steady work for the coming year. He was also convinced that
Daddy was desperate for his arrival, because Daddy wanted to pay
the fare for Pippin and his family to get there.

About a month later, I received a letter from Mama letting
me know that all was well with Pippin and his family. James and
the other croppers had made them feel right at home and their
children, although behind on several areas of schoolwork, eagerly
looked forward to every assignment set before them. Mama said
Pippin was especially happy to learn that he would receive a full
cash share of the cotton that would come in for the year, as much
of it had been planted by the families who had moved off to
Conecuh County, anyway. Her letter went on to let me know how
she, Daddy, and Jess were all doing and what kinds of responses

had been received from the letters we sent out regarding Daddy's run for the state senate. I could tell by Mama's words that she was tired and looked forward to my return to Melrose School, where I would do my internship. It was something I was eager to do, knowing that once I completed it, I'd receive my teaching certificate and would be able to start living my dream of being a teacher. First, though, before I started teaching others, it seemed that God had a message that he wanted me to hear, and luckily, I paid attention.

Like most folks, I was always looking forward to something happening in the future. Whether it was going to college for the first time or finishing up so I could teach, there seemed to always be that something down the road that would make me happy and content. But then after hearing a sermon Professor Clayton preached one Sunday, I was hit between the eyes of what I had been guilty of my whole life.

"Did you know that God has numbered all of your days," Professor Clayton said to the congregation, "and this bein the case, why do we often think that tomorrow will be better than today or when this or that happens all will be well? The truth is that God has given you each day as a gift and none are to be wasted or overlooked. Now, don't get me wrong, cause I look forward to lots of things myself, like goin fishin, for instance, or like when my children were born. No, the kinda things I'm talkin about are those that make you think that when they finally happen, you will be satisfied in this life. Don't waste your time thinkin like that, folks. Pay attention to where you are right now, thank God for each day he gives you, and quit lookin off down the road so much. If you'll start practicing this, I promise that you will not only be much more content with your life, but you will also be a blessin to others as well."

Just how many times had I overlooked something or somebody I didn't know? To be truthful, I was even scared to think about it much. I did know it would have been easy to overlook Pippin, though, especially if God hadn't of put him in front of me the way he did. I thought a lot about that. I also thought of how I had gotten up before daylight that morning to pray for his situation and the difference it seemed to make when the world was quiet and still. I remembered how Professor Carver had shared those very thoughts in Tuskegee that night, and the difference praying in the morning made to him. He had done it for years, and in spite of all the hardships he suffered in life, he seemed to be one of the most content people I had ever met. I was also curious about something: I knew that when I prayed I was talking to God, but I had never considered the fact that God might want to talk to me, also. Professor Carver was the first person I had ever met who claimed that God actually yearned to talk with all of us. After I had considered the whole matter for a while, I felt that I should also make it a habit of meeting with God in the silence and solitude of the morning; and once I did, I quickly realized that God had been patiently waiting on me to do just that.

Chapter 17

The Wedding

The election for the state senate seats were held in mid-November, and it seemed that all the hard work Mama and I had done indeed paid off. Daddy won his district by a large margin of votes, and in January 1914 in Montgomery, he would be sworn into office as Senator Dison Winford Taylor, representing the people of Coffee, Pike, and parts of Dale Counties, Alabama, for the next four years. I was excited for Daddy and was congratulated on his behalf by many of the folks who patronized Byrd's Apothecary. I knew my father was a good and honest man who helped others when it was within his power to do so, and now he had a bigger opportunity to do even more of that. I remember hearin him say several times how good deeds seemed to find their way back to the unselfish; not that he did good deeds for the sake of reward, but more as if it was a law of return that God had set up and we were all expected to follow.

I was also happy that Daddy would have a new source of income, because the businesses of growing and ginning cotton were sure to be impeded once the boll weevil made it to our area. I still prayed about that and held out a high hope that somehow, somewhere, someone would come up with a poison that would wipe them all out. That was the most logical thing I could think of happening, and after bringing this petition before God once again, a particular verse in the Book of Psalms jumped out at me that morning. It was in Chapter 77:19 and read "Your road led through the sea, your pathway through the mighty waters, a pathway no one knew was there." That morning, two things became clear to me: One was that God had been hearing my prayers all along about the situation. The second was a peaceful realization that I needed to just wait and see how God's will would unfold concerning the matter.

When I returned home, it was once again close to Christmas. The cotton had all been gathered by the end of October and as expected, yielded better than average because of the snow we had received the year before. James had managed the gin and its customers well while Daddy had been politicking, and Jess had managed the chores around the house without running away again or fussing too much. It was good to be back at Melrose with my family, especially during my favorite time of year. I also knew Sipsey would be home soon, too, which made it all the more exciting.

The day after I had gotten back, we were surprised by a knock on the door not long after we had finished breakfast. It was Pippin and his wife Bonnie Kate.

"We don't want to bother y'all. Just wanted to drop by for a minute on our way to town," Pippin said as they came inside.

After several minutes of small talk, Pippin said, "Miss Janie, I just wanted to thank you for what you done for me and mine. Meetin you the way I did in Troy and comin here was the best thing that could a happened for all of us."

"Well, Pippin, I'm glad it has worked out," I said, "and Daddy was just now tellin me how handy you've been on building rooms on all the rail cars, somethin I know all the ladies must appreciate."

"I might as well be doin somethin, cause it's shore hard for me to set still anyway," he said as Bonnie Kate nodded and rolled her eyes. "Well, we just wanted to stop by and letchall know we've put off the idea of goin to South Carolina for now. We've been made to feel right at home by ever body, and for the time bein, this is where we need to be."

After saying goodbye, Pippin and Bonnie Kate headed on into town.

Later that afternoon, they came back by, and this time Sipsey was riding with them. It was so good to see her smiling face, and once Pippin had dropped her off, Sipsey and I went inside to eat some Christmas cookies Mama and I had made. We spent the next couple of hours visiting and catching up, and durin that time Sipsey surprised me with some special news.

"I wanted you to be the first to know, Janie," Sipsey began as I eased forward in anticipation of her surprise. "When I finish school this year, I'm gonna be gettin married, and if my fiancé's accepted into medical school in New York, that's where we're gonna be livin for the next good little while."

I was shocked and knew Sipsey could tell by the look that must have been all over my face.

"I've been knowin Rodney since last year, but we just started courtin about a month ago," she said with a huge smile and batting her eyelids in a way I had never seen her do before. "I would have told you in a letter, but figured it'd be best to just wait and surprise you in person with it. Rodney knows I want to be married before I move off anywhere with him, and he's vowed to do the proper thing. We plan on havin the weddin in the chapel at Tuskegee, and I want you to be there as my witness when we do."

"Well, of course I will, Sipsey!" I said with honor and excitement. "You're my best friend and I'd be honored to stand with you."

Then after talking a while longer, we hitched up the buggy and rode on over so she could tell her daddy the news.

"Lawd, have mercy, girl," Sipsey's daddy said, shaking his head. "I knowed bettern to letchoo go off to that school in the fust place. Now my baby gone run off up Nawth somewhere and forget she ever even had a daddy!" Then, putting his arm around her shoulders, he pulled his daughter close and kissed her on the head. "I guess we'll all manage somehow," he said, holding his back as if he'd been carrying the whole load by himself. "Maybe yo husband can help my rheumatism somehow when he starts doctorin." We all giggled.

Sipsey and Rodney were married in late Spring, and as promised, I stood by her side. Rodney seemed to be a very kind and attentive person and paid particular mind to Sipsey's family before and after the wedding. I had met him briefly once before, being introduced as an assistant to Booker T. Washington, President of Tuskegee Institute, and Rodney had asked him to stand as his best man. I was delighted to have finally met President Washington after hearing so much about him for the past two years. I also met Rodney's family, who were all very polite and seemed to be well off by the way they were dressed and carried themselves in conversation. This was also the first time Daddy had the chance to meet my friend Professor Carver.

"Professor, I wanted to thank you for sendin me those pamphlets about crop rotation," Daddy said. "I was amazed at our cotton yield this last year, and I got several other folks believin in the practice of doin the same thing in their own fields now."

"I am so glad to hear that, Senator," Professor Carver replied. "I just wish more folks would understand the importance of doin this very thing. Course lots of them say they don't have the acreage to do so, but like I have said to them before, what difference does it make if half your land produces twice as much? By the way, I wanted to ask you what your colleagues in Montgomery are sayin about the boll weevil infestation that is headin our way."

"It has come up several times now," Daddy said, "especially by those who own land and have a vested interest in cotton like I do, but yes, we have talked at length with the head of the state agriculture department, and like everyone else, he seems to be at a loss as to how the issue will be resolved. My personal opinion is that it will be a good while before anything is figured out on how to stop them. Of course, it goes without sayin that our economy is gonna be devastated just like the other states that have been hit, but ya know, I think it's time we came up with somethin besides cotton to make our livin on anyway." Then, whispering so that only Professor Carver and I could hear it, Daddy said, "But God help the man who offers that as a solution or shouts it from a rooftop anywhere in the South, for if he did, he might as well volunteer himself to be hung by a mob."

"I know exactly what you mean," Professor Carver said, laughing. "But let us pray to that end anyway, for history reveals that all kings may face the chance of being overthrown, and King Cotton is long overdue."

I admired my father for what he had said. Here was a man who had depended on cotton to make his living and take care of his family for years, but at the same time, he was big enough to admit there needed to be a change in how that was done.

After everyone had visited for a while longer, the pastor had us all line up so that Rodney and Sipsey could say their goodbyes. When Sipsey made it up to where I was, she promised to write as soon as she could and to come visit as often as possible. Then with tears welling up in her eyes, she asked me to give Pastor Seth a message the very next time I saw him.

"I want you to tell him I said thank you for that sermon he preached when we first came to Melrose, and tell him thank you for that night at your house, too. I know for sure if none of that had happened, I wouldn't have come to this school and I wouldn't be getting married today. I've already thanked God for what happened back then, but I never told Pastor Seth thank you, and I want you to tell him for me."

Then after hugging her daddy and brothers for a long time, Sipsey headed out the door for New York, a married woman.

Chapter 18

The Boll Weevil Cometh

For the most part, 1915 started out not so differently from the year before. I returned to my teaching at Melrose School. Daddy returned to traveling back to Montgomery with Mama in tow. Mama took care of all the details that Daddy claimed did nothing but tangle up his brains. As far as our family went, the biggest change was with Jess. Mama and Daddy felt he needed more challenge and structure in his life, so they enrolled him at Lyman Ward Military Academy at Camp Hill, Alabama, something he finally admitted he looked forward to. The croppers and farmers across the county planted their fields the same as always, with each one holding onto the hope that the little bug that had already been wreaking havoc in other parts of the state would be kind enough to hold off another year – or better yet, just pass us by altogether. Instead, though, they found their cotton crops to be all but devastated. Up until that time, Daddy's ginning business had turned out an average of 35,000 bales of cotton per season. After the crops were ravished that year, they had only 14,000, a loss of sixty percent. The loss for the entire Cotton Belt was much more staggering. By 1922, it was estimated that tens of millions of dollars had been lost to the boll-weevil infestation, affecting millions of people directly and indirectly.

"Well, it ain't like we didn't know this wad'nt gone happen," James said one evening as he and the other men sat drinking coffee.

"Oh, yeah," Pippin said, "and I'm here to tell y'all it ain't gone get no better, neither. You'd be lucky if you get enough cotton to stuff yer mattress with next year."

"Gets to where I hate to read the newspaper anymore," James said. "Seems like it's just filled up with nothin but hard luck stories, and I hear enough a them from customers at the gin. I guess we ought to be thankful though, thankful we still got plenty to et. If'n it was the other way around and this plague got all the food crops, it'd shore be hard to chew up and swallow that cotton."

One day not long after the gin had closed for the season, James came by and approached Daddy with an opportunity the croppers had been mulling over. Seems Pippin had received a post from his brother in South Carolina. His employer was making plans to expand his peanut acreage, and he needed more croppers to plant and harvest the crops there. Pippin, from experience, had convinced them all that cotton was done for now, but would vouch for any family that wanted to pull up stakes and head with him to South Carolina. James, who had grown close to Daddy over the years, wanted to hear Daddy's thoughts before his mind was made up on what to do.

"I tell you, James," Daddy said, "if'n I was in your shoes, I'm not sure I wouldn't be a lookin ahead just like you are. I'm not gonna argue with ya and say next year we'd be back on track with our cotton, cause I don't think we will be. From what I have gathered from all the agricultural folks, we ain't any closer to killin off that bug than the Pea River is of flowin backwards. Truth is, I been worried about every one a y'all. I know there's plenty to eat and y'all ain't gonna starve to death, but I also know there's more to life than just eatin. A man wants to have somethin to show for his hard work. So I say if you like all the details Pippin is tellin y'all, I wouldn't fault cha a bit about goin on up there." Then after pausing for a second, Daddy said, "Y'all can sell off the mules and milk cows and even the chickens, and that oughta more than cover your train tickets."

After James had sat there awhile nodding his head, he seemed to finally find the words he was lookin for.

"Winford, you are one of the best friends I ever had. You and your family have done nothin but right by every one of us." Then wiping a tear, he continued speaking, "There ain't no way I could ever repay you for your kindness, but I give ya my word: I will do my best to pass that same kinda charity on to someone else."

"That's fair enough for me," Daddy said. And with that, the two old friends shook hands.

A few weeks later we all gathered to say our goodbyes. There were tears from both sides of the fence, for we all knew it was unlikely we'd ever see one another again. It had been a little over ten years now since the sharecropper families had first arrived at Melrose Plantation, not one of them knowing what to expect. Now, each family was leaving for South Carolina able to read and write and also handle almost any type of mathematical problem they might encounter. Many of them vowed to look for land of their own once they had saved up a little more, and even went as far to say they'd come back to Melrose if the cotton situation got better. Sipsey's father and I spoke for a good little while, and he felt if nothing else, they would be closer to each other and it might mean getting to see her more often. After we had all spent most the afternoon together, James asked if we could come and gather in front of the school to pray. We all bowed our heads, and those who wanted to said a little prayer. Then after the last person finished, Jess, on his own, had the wits to ring the bell. For Melrose School, it would be for the very last time.

Chapter 19

Sipsey's New Home

I guess New York was about as far from the South as a soul could get. Not that I was trying to get away from there, but just noticed what a different world I was living in now. Seems like people were always moving around and wanting to hitch a ride somewhere. It reminded me of cuckle burrs on a dogs tail. And the streets were all one on top of another too. They had started building the subways in 1904, and I had ridden on them several times now and didn't have any use for them. People crowding in there every which a way and hollering out like Benny use to do. I remember the day before our wedding Rodney telling my brother Spookie that there was over four million people where he and I would be moving. Spookie just nodded his head like he already knew about the place and then wanting to add something to the conversation, asked "what ch'all 'specting in cotton up there this next go round?"

In spite of all the changes, I decided early on I wouldn't fret about things. I had already done too much of that when I was younger, and figured if God could see me through those times He would help me with any troubles I set before Him. It made things easier on Rodney too. I knew he was worried I might get all sulled up and maybe want to be moving back south.

I did miss my family though, but knew it would probably be awhile before either one of us could count on a visit. Daddy had written to tell me they would be moving with the other croppers to South Carolina. He went on to explain how "dat bug has ben eatin up de cotton" at Melrose and they would be going into the peanut business. I remembered the talk about the boll weevil. Many places had already suffered from its wrath and now it had made its way into Alabama. I also had a dream the night after getting daddy's letter. It was about Granny Moss, and she was putting one of her superstitions on me. In my dream she pointed out to the cotton fields she had been working in and said "Um huh. I knew dem white folks wuz gwanna pay fo dat big stack a wrongs they been a doin." Then after moving around to get a better look at the bugs she stood up and pointed over to the right side of the fields. "You sees 'em don't cha? Dey de ones what done dropped 'em in de fields. Dey de ghost slaves." In my dream I never saw the ghosts but knew what she meant. The spirits of the dead slaves, those who had once been forced to work the plantations, were getting retribution by dropping the boll weevils in the cotton fields. It sounded just like something she would have come up with.

Janie and I had also written each other several times after I had first gotten here and from what I could piece together she and her family were all tolerable. In my first letter to her I told her all about New York, including my excitement in visiting the Statue of Liberty, something Miz Anna had us all learn about while at Melrose School. I went on to tell her what a big adjustment it was moving here, but also gave her plenty to laugh about. The last thing I wanted was for her or anyone else to be fretting on my account.

As far as hearing from home folks, Rodney and I had a pleasant surprise one evening that we would come to treasure forever. Booker T. Washington, President of Tuskegee Institute came by our apartment in late October of 1915. He was in New York doing his usual speaking and fund raising for the Institute and decided to hunt us up for a visit. It was so good to see him, and we spent the better part of four hours eating, laughing and getting caught up on news from Tuskegee. He was also a great encouragement in regards to my quest in finding a teaching job saying, "Sipsey, God has gifted you for a reason. He has called you to be a teacher, and I have no doubt you will bless many with your calling before you leave this earth. Be patient. God will open a door for you when it is time." Then later, while bidding us farewell, he paused on our steps. Looking up at me he said, "You know Sipsey, God placed a calling on my life many years ago also; I feel now, I have fought the good fight and I have run the good race."

Three weeks later Rodney and I were both devastated to learn Dr. Washington had collapsed while still here in New York,

and though taken to a hospital, the treatment he received was
ineffective. He then requested to be taken back to Tuskegee where
he died on November 14th.

Rodney and I both wanted to attend his funeral. We were
making plans to head back to Alabama that week until we both
came down with the flu and thought death would visit us also. By
the time we had gotten well enough to travel, it was too late. Not to
be out done by our circumstances though, we put together a little
memorial for him one night, and said our own goodbyes. We
pinned a photograph of Dr. Washington, one we cut from the
newspaper, on the wall and lit a candle next to it. There we sat and
through tears recalled some of the personal moments we had spent
with him. Rodney had been his student assistant while at Tuskegee
and then in turn, Dr. Washington had stood as Rodney's best man at
our wedding. I on the other hand had gotten to know him when I
stayed in Tuskegee one summer and took care of his home while
he traveled. After he returned, he was delighted at how well I had
taken care of things. He would then from time to time invite me to
serve at some of the faculty events. Once telling the teachers,
within my ear shot "I hope one day this young lady from Melrose
School will join us here in what we are trying to get
accomplished."

As far as my old school, it saddened me to hear it was
closed now. It was such a huge blessing in my life, and a big part
of the reason why I was here in New York, happily married and
about to start a full-time teaching job. Though I had substituted at
two of the negro schools already, I was convinced it would be
awhile before I found a permanent position at either one of them,
which is what I wanted. I was about to give up on that notion when
I was approached by the head of one of the schools and asked if I
would be interested in being the teacher for a new class they were
creating. It would consist of twelve students who needed special
attention. They varied in age and grade, but all needed to catch up
on their learning. Some of the students had had very little
instruction before, while others had fallen behind for one reason or
another. I jumped at the opportunity. I knew it would be a
challenge, but I was ready. My job was to get them caught up, and

I knew the faculty's eyes would be on me. As far as what was offered to black students in 1915 in New York City, this school was considered the most prominent source of education. Much of our funding came from the private donations of businesses and wealthy individuals, and I knew how important it was to . . . please them.

I remembered many of the methods Miz Anna used with us at Melrose and knew they had worked well. I implemented these and some variations. My students practiced reading out loud every day and as part of their homework I instructed each one to write a short essay every other week on something from the newspaper that interested them. I also had them doing something one of my professors at Tuskegee had done and that was increasing their vocabulary by giving out seldom-used words from a *Webster's Dictionary*. Each student was given a different word, and it was to be used in sentences daily for a week. Of course there were some students who were so far behind in their reading, writing, and mathematical abilities that they couldn't be expected to do such things right away. I kept my patience though and progress was made. As the school year ended I was approached once again and this time asked to teach adult classes at night and during the summer months. I was also asked to take over one of the regular classrooms in the fall. God had opened that door.

My plate was full now and Rodney stayed busy as well with his studies. All along I would find myself making a new friend, and New York began to feel much more like home. I was embracing the opportunities God had for me here and before long, knew without a doubt I wanted to spend my life living in this city. I still missed my family, but Daddy, after receiving several letters from me, finally agreed he and my brothers would come visit us when their next harvest was done. I was hungry to see them. I also wanted to see the look on Spookie's face when I showed him all the sights

As for Janie, I knew she was busy with her teaching just like I was. Our letters to each other became sporadic, but I always kept her in my prayers. As a matter of fact that's where I kept all the folks I loved.

Chapter 20

Men of Vision

The following year was even worse on those who chose to continue growing cotton. Close to ninety percent of what was grown in our area was utterly devoured by what came to be known as "the meanest little bug in America." There was, however, something in the works that if successful, would give the farmers in our county some hope.

Professor Carver wrote me a letter shortly before the upcoming planting season had started. In it, he confessed he had no sure sign as to why he should lay such information at my feet other than a strong inclination from God to do so. He went on to inform me that the impressions he had shared with me previously about growing peanuts were confirmed early one morning as he sat quietly by himself asking for some kind of direction for the farmers around Tuskegee.

"I don't know if you can do anything with what I have shared with you here," he said in his letter, "but with your father being a state senator for that area, he might have influences on certain people who would only scoff if the advice came directly from me. But regardless, if they are smart, I think it would be best for them to plant their fields in peanuts and if so, we will trust God to do the rest."

After reading Professor Carver's letter, the first thing that came to my mind was a dream that I'd had just the night before. I was at Troy Normal again and many of the students were at a picnic celebrating the end of the school year. Besides the food, we also had different games we were playing. In my dream, I participated in several of the contests, with most of them being designed to do no more than bring about a good fit of laughter. The last contest, however, was a relay race and in this one, my demeanor seemed to be much more serious. I was running with the baton, and although I had never been very fast, I was determined to put my teammate in the best possible position to win. As I rounded my last bend, the ground I was running on changed from grass into a freshly plowed field and although the going was much slower, I was more than bound to deliver that baton. After struggling for what seemed like an hour to get through the soft dirt, I finally found myself on the other side of the field, exhausted but surprised that there was no one single person to hand the baton off to, but rather hundreds of people, all with their hands out and all of them eagerly waiting. Once I received and read the words of Professor Carver's letter, I knew the pages I held not only had my good friend's finger prints on them, but God's as well.

That evening after Daddy and Mama had gotten back home from town, I shared with them the letter I had received as well as the dream I'd had the night before.

"I'd say that dream you had is every bit as powerful as the one your mama had bout startin that school for the croppers," Daddy said. "And I trust your friend Professor Carver, too. If he says God has told him something, I have no reason to doubt it one bit." Then after reading the letter for himself, Daddy nodded his head a few times and said, "Janie, if you'll give me a day or two, I'm confident I will have some folks to hand this information off to, and when I do, I want you to be there with me."

Two days later, we hitched the wagon and headed to town. The day before, Daddy had met with John Pittman, the county agriculture agent, and asked him if he knew anyone who would be willing to try an experiment, one that just might help our local economy. Mr. Pittman was assured he knew such a man of vision and told Daddy what hour to be at his office the next day. When we arrived, sure enough, there was a man in his office – one Daddy had met on several occasions but had never done any type of business with. His name was H.M. Sessions. Although Mr. Sessions was not originally from our county, he had been in Enterprise for several years now, bringing a considerable amount of knowledge about the banking industry with him and making numerous loans to the people in our area, many of whom were farmers. All the reports Daddy had heard about him were good, and Daddy felt comfortable revealing his thoughts to him.

"I like the idea, Senator," he said right off. "I have heard that there's farmers in other states who make a good livin doin nothin but raisin peanuts for the seed, and I think that'd be our best bet too. You know like a distributor, where we'd be promotin and sellin to farmers and seed stores. The question is, with it bein so late in the plantin season, we may only find one or two with enough to fill our needs, and then they're gonna know right off we'll be goin into business against them—somethin they probably won't like."

Up until that time, I had only been listening to the conversation, but once Mr. Sessions had finished putting forth his thoughts on the matter, I spoke up.

"Mr. Sessions, if you will let me know how many peanuts are needed to get this whole thing started, I will wire a good friend of mine in South Carolina," I said, "and if they have the seeds, they'll ship 'em here with no questions asked."

"Well, all right, then!" Mr. Sessions said, laughing and slapping the desk. "Give me a few days and I'll have a number for you. If your friend can supply our needs, I'll go to South Carolina and pay for 'em and then escort the little goobers back."

After we left Mr. Pittman's office and started back home, Daddy looked at me and smiled. "You're about to call in some favors, aren't cha?" he asked with a chuckle.

"I sure am, Daddy, and I don't think God or anybody else will fault me for it, do you?" I asked.

"Of course not!" Daddy replied. "I was just thinkin what a good politician you'd make."

Several days later, Mr. Sessions gave me an approximate number of seeds he needed. I then sent a Western Union telegraph to Pippin in South Carolina.

"Need enough peanut seed to plant 300 acres. STOP. Man will pay cash and escort the shipment home. STOP Consider this a personal favor. STOP Signed Janie Taylor"

Late the next day I received my reply.

"Consider the favor done. STOP Tell your man they are waiting on his arrival. STOP"

The day after I received Pippin's wire, Mr. Sessions headed to South Carolina. Then a little over a week later, he returned with the seed and a letter to me from Pippin.

Dear Miss Janie,

I hope this post finds you well. Ther's hardly a day goes by you or yore family is not brung up in conversation by one of us. When I first approached Mr. Winsley about yore needs he flat out refused sayin if'n he got ya started growin and sellin peanuts down there and wurd got out he'd shore nuff be horse whipped by the folks in his association. The next day though me and James Quincy and the rest of the folks ya know hear told him we wadn't gonna hit another lick 'till he agreed to fill the order and we meant it to. After seein what it meant to us he told me to go wire ya back. He is mostly a good and God fearin man but needs to be mule kicked ever so often. Please give my regards to everyone.

Pippin

Along with the seed, Mr. Sessions had also obtained from Pippin information on proper planting methods. He had already lined up a handful of farmers to plant the seeds before he had left, and Mr. C.W. Baston took the lead by agreeing to plant one hundred twenty-five acres. He had approached many others in hopes that it would increase the scale of the experiment we had started, but found that regardless of the boll weevil infestation the previous year, most of the farmers had planted their fields in cotton once again, hoping for a bumper crop this time to make up for the past losses and to cover the notes held by the banks.

Not long after the seeds were planted, I found myself from time to time having fears that what I had started might come to naught. After all, no one had ever grown this amount of acreage in peanuts in our area before. We also had no buyers lined up as of yet and didn't know for sure if we would. After this panic had weighed on me for the better part of a week, I found a quiet place where I could pray and hopefully get some resolve for what I was feeling. After several moments of prayer, I opened my Bible, not having any particular place in mind, and began reading in Proverbs. I had not gone far when the first sentence in Chapter 11, Verse 11 spoke clearly to my fears: "By the blessings of the upright a city is exalted" I immediately knew in my heart what God was conveying to me. He had not turned a deaf ear to my prayers, but had heard each and every one of them, and I felt that by His hand our lives would be blessed.

Shortly after our experiment had started, I penned a letter to Professor Carver and assured him that I had received his post and said exactly how his advice was now being implemented for our area. I did not go into the details about my dream or anything else God had shown me, figuring I would tell him in person the next chance I had to see him.

Chapter 21

An Unfolded Blessing

It was now late August, and I was preparing to teach at Mossy Grove School outside of Troy. The former teacher had retired at the end of the previous school year and had contacted me about meeting with the Pike County Education Board as her replacement. We had first met by way of Aunt Julia, who had taught with the former teacher at Troy Normal, and subsequently I conversed with her on several occasions during my employment at Byrd's Apothecary.

Melrose was a good thirty miles from Mossy Grove, and I had the option of making that trip each day, which would take almost two hours by buggy; or I could move into some side rooms that had been built onto the school house. After going back and forth the first couple of days, I decided it'd be best to gather my things and make the school my home, at least during the week.

Although I was now busy with teaching, the experiment that was implemented was never far from my mind, and because I was the one who had brought the idea of growing peanuts to Coffee County, I kept in contact with Mr. Sessions as much as possible. The seeds he had brought back were planted in late May, and from the information Pippin had given him, they needed 120 to 140 days before they would be ready for harvest. It was something each one of us was eagerly anticipating.

On October 28, 1916, Mr. Baston arrived in Enterprise with mules and wagons carrying 8,000 bushels of peanuts. It was a Saturday, and by chance I happened to be in town completing several errands that Daddy had assigned Mama and me to do. Mr. Baston was sitting on the lead wagon and seeing me out on the walkway, took his straw hat off, showed me a huge grin and then bowed as he went by. The excitement I felt at that moment was overwhelming. My first thought was to take off running and follow him straight to Mr. Sessions' office. However, knowing I had invested nothing financially into the venture, I reconsidered, feeling I might be out of place by doing so. Besides that, I didn't know if Mama's heart would hold up seeing her now-grown daughter running lickety-split through town with her dress hiked up.

The information I received about the first transaction of peanuts came from Daddy, who later that week had gone by to see him. Mr. Sessions had agreed beforehand to pay Mr. Baston one dollar per bushel when delivered, which was a fair price considering he had fronted him the seeds, the fertilizer, and the machinery to plant and harvest the crop. Although the plans he first expressed were to become a distributor, selling the seeds outside Enterprise, a new man of vision had promptly stepped up with an offer that caused the entire venture to practically explode overnight. Mr. R. C. Conner, a friend and business associate of Daddy's who owned the local cottonseed oil company, guaranteed every farmer in the area a market for their upcoming crops, no matter how big or small. Up until that time Mr. Conner had always sold every bit of the cottonseed oil he had produced year in and year out, but knowing how cotton was being hurt the way it was, he knew there would need to be a replacement. Peanut oil would do nicely, he believed.

The whole countryside was now abuzz by what had just happened, many thinking Mr. Conner had overstepped with his promises and would not be able to honor the contracts he had signed. But shortly thereafter, and as God would have it, word began spreading by mouth and newspaper that a Negro college professor who taught agriculture at Tuskegee Institute had just discovered six new uses for the peanut — something that quickly hushed the naysayers and made the peanut market much more promising.

The following year, the production and sales of the peanut was almost beyond belief, with the farmers in Coffee County harvesting more than one million bushels and grossing more than five million dollars in revenue. This was much higher than any other county in the United States, and farmers quickly realized that one acre of peanuts would bring in more money than one acre of cotton.

I continued seeing newspaper reports of how much our local economy had improved; the same conclusion could easily be read in how the people now carried themselves. It was hard to believe that only two years before, many of these same folks had faced bankruptcy. Worry was written on their faces from the time they awoke in the morning until they went to bed at night, with sleep giving them very little escape from their thoughts. These were honest people who paid their debts and stood behind the word they gave to others. The plague of the boll weevil had left them perplexed and beside themselves, not knowing which way to turn. I had begun seeing the same look on people's faces that I had seen on Pippin's when I first met him in Troy. True, most of the folks in our county hadn't lost their homes or moved off yet, but they all knew if relief didn't come soon, it'd just be a matter of time.

Now, though, by virtue of this unfolded blessing, old debts were being paid off; money was spent freely in the shops and stores again; people were walking with a spring in their step and bright smiles on their faces; and the offering plates at the churches were being filled. It was as if a terrible curse had been lifted from our land, and now a spirit of gladness had taken its place.

Word spread quickly throughout the Cotton Kingdom of what had happened in our little county in South Alabama. Now farmers in Texas, Arkansas, Louisiana, Mississippi, Georgia, and north Florida, as well as in other Alabama counties began planting their once-ravished fields in peanuts. The market continued to be strong, mainly because of the new uses for the peanut that were constantly being discovered by Professor Carver, some of which our government began implementing to feed our troops, who had just entered the war against Germany.

Everyone had been keeping up with what was going on overseas, and all had felt America would be involved sooner or later. The thing that bothered me most, of course, was that Jess was now 16 years old and enrolled in a military school. I knew that if the war lasted another year or so, he would be enlisted into the armed services with a good chance of being right in the thick of it.

Later when we did enter the war, President Wilson asked for every citizen in our country to make an effort, supplying our boys and the government with all types of necessities. I felt my part could best be done in the form of fund raising, and because I had created a drama club at Mossy Grove School, I decided we should put on several plays to raise money for our troops. Often we had done *Old Salty Dog*, the same play I had helped write and produce at Troy Normal, but when invited by Pastor Seth to bring our group to perform at my church homecoming in Enterprise, I decided it would be more appropriate to present a new play I had written based on one of my favorite books in the Bible, the story of Esther. We had only two weeks before our performance, and I began working right away to help the students learn their parts for each scene. After many hours of hard work and preparation and feeling as though everything had finally come together, Bethany Lee, who was set to play the lead character, came down with a horrible case of the chicken pox, something that was usually visited on children well before they had reached her age. I was quite flustered by this new predicament. With the homecoming date set in stone, it was out of the question to replace Bethany's part with anyone else, except of course for me, who knew the lines by heart. So knowing what had to be done I called for two more rehearsals to practice my timing and voice inflection. The second rehearsal was finished only moments before we were to leave by automobile for our destination. Melrose, thank goodness, was on the way and I asked that we leave in plenty of time so I could recruit Mama to help me with my costume and hair. After all was completed there, we headed for our new production. As we left Mama's, my hair was in large ringlets which draped over my shoulders; I wore a flowing white gown, and the golden head band, which signified my status as a queen, rested securely across my lap. After we arrived and had eaten and visited for a little while, we all excused ourselves to begin setting up a makeshift stage. An hour later and when Pastor Seth had been signaled, the play programs were handed out to an audience that filled the pews from front to back. The church had been wired for electricity now and all the lights were turned off except for those up front, which made a good setting for our production. The way I had written the play, it was to last not much over an hour, with the end being the verse in Chapter 4, Verse 14, where Esther realized how God had placed her in the position of queen so that her people could be saved.

After the play was finished and the applause had stopped, we found ourselves to be under time restraints from our driver, who did not see well at night, so we quickly loaded into the automobile and headed back to Mossy Grove. It was in late May when we held the performance, our final one for the year and the one and only time *Esther* was ever presented on stage.

Chapter 22

For Such a Time as This

It seems the years of my life had gone by way too fast, with only certain moments in time, frozen here and there. In my late twenties, I married, only to become widowed and childless after fifteen short years. Mama and Daddy, who had both been so beloved by me, died in 1945 and 1946, not quite eight months apart. They were buried at Melrose Plantation, just beyond where the rail cars had once stood and within earshot of the Pea River. Jess crossed an ocean when he was only eighteen, but by the time he had made it to the war, it was over within a month's time. After several more years in the service, he eventually mustered out and moved to Dothan, where he lived and worked and showed some political ambition by running for city council, an office he won each time and held for a number of terms. Sispey and I wrote back and forth over the years, but as fate would have it, we never had the opportunity to see one another again. Our only consolation was to hear each others' voices by telephone from time to time. I also stayed in touch with Professor Carver until he died in 1943, having the privilege once to spend several hours visiting with him at Tuskegee again, talking about various things, including the many uses he had found for the peanut, which eventually grew to more than three hundred and included such things as shaving cream, mayonnaise, glue, hand lotion, rubber, and plastic. Besides my father and late husband, there was no one man I respected more and thought of so often, remembering one instance in particular when I visited with him in Dothan before the annual Peanut Festival there. Several people were making a fuss over a float that was to be in the parade that day, and Professor Carver, who was now in his seventies and watching it all, slapped his leg in laughter and said, "Lawd Janie! Look what we done got started with our peanuts."

After almost twenty years of teaching, I left my position at Mossy Grove School for an admissions job at Troy State Teachers College, as my *alma mater* Troy Normal School had come to be known. With Jess and me both busy with our lives and careers, we figured it best to rent out the eight hundred acres of farmland that had been left to us, but kept the old home place at Melrose Plantation for our personal use. At different times, we each made visits to Melrose to relax and walk once again the steps of our youth, and always kept our pledge for his family and me to gather there at Christmas, hoping with each occasion, that we would once again be blessed with snow.

After several years and on one such visit, I discovered an old trunk of mine that Mama had stored away long before. I remembered the trunk, but unable to find its key anywhere, I loaded it into my car thinking I could somehow get it open when I got home.

Although I had lived in Troy for the last thirty years, I continued to keep up with all the events of my hometown of Enterprise by maintaining my subscription to their newspaper. The most recent edition I had received showed where my old church was having its homecoming once again on the upcoming Sunday with Pastor Seth, who was now in his late seventies and retired, delivering the message for that day. I decided the minute I read the article that I must attend that event. It had been such a long time since I had visited my old church and now being the month of May, I could also treat myself by stopping at Melrose to visit my favorite spots there and do any maintenance that needed to be done around Mama's and Daddy's grave sites. With that chore in mind and knowing how forgetful I could be, I went out to the shed behind my house to get the rake and hoe I would need. Then after moving several items around to get to them, I noticed the still-unopened trunk I had sat on a small table in the corner that December when I had gotten back home. Once I had loaded my tools, I dusted off the trunk and took it into the house, determined this time to somehow get it open. After spending a good thirty minutes and havin no success unlocking it, I left it sitting where it was, at least satisfied that I now had the thing inside.

It was now Saturday evening, and knowing I would be leaving early the next morning for the homecoming event, I packed some extra clothes I'd need and then refrigerated the food I had prepared. After all was finished, I finally settled into the bed, where I always read for awhile before going to sleep. I had been trying to get interested in one particular book for over a week now, but not having much hope that it would get any better, decided instead to read a few chapters in my Bible, something I now did only sporadically. Over the years, I had not made an effort on my personal studies of God's word, and even though I still went to church regularly and often prayed, my spiritual life did not have the same heartfelt sincerity of my younger days. I had lost the habit of rising early in the morning, when I would seek and often hear God's voice, something I yearned for once again but did not put forth the effort to receive. The fact that I no longer had this type of fellowship with God disturbed me now to the point that I wanted to know why. So that night, on my knees, I asked God as sincerely as I could to show me where I might have gone wrong.

After my prayer, I drifted off into one of the most restful sleeps I had had in years. I awoke at 4:30 the next morning, made my usual pot of coffee, and sat enjoying the first cup. As I drank, I remembered thinking how spry I felt from the good night's rest and at age 54, how well I usually felt from day to day. Aside from lack of sleep sometimes and a trick knee, I had no health problems I was aware of. It was while these thoughts crossed my mind that I once again noticed the little trunk I had brought inside the day before, sitting right where I had left it by the kitchen door. As I eyed the aggravating lock, it dawned on me that it was not a key lock, but a trick lock. The plate had a key hole that was fake and it was something you simply pushed to one side and then mashed a button, which would then open the trunk. It had been a gift from James Quincy's wife Isabel over thirty years before during Christmas, and right before they had all left for South Carolina. I had only used it on a few occasions, I remembered, because I had other trunks I preferred that held more of the necessities I usually needed. Knowing this, Mama had put this one away in a place I never thought to look, and it wasn't until Jess's family and I had all gathered for Christmas that I found it when we were hiding Santa Claus gifts for his kids.

Now that I remembered how the lock worked, I pulled my chair over and just as I thought, opened it like I had the very last time, which was shortly after the Esther play some twenty-eight years before. On top was the little tray that was designed to hold papers or valuables. In mine, I found the pocket knife Mr. Byrd had given me, which had first belonged to my great-great grandfather and had then been dropped through the little crack by Uncle Russell before he had gone off to fight the Yankees in 1861. I also found, to my surprise, the little wooden angel James had carved for me as a Christmas gift, something I treasured but thought had been lost forever since I had not seen it in such a long time.

There was also a large envelope with the play program, some newspaper clippings I paid no attention to right then, and a little diary I had rarely used over the years. These I decided to take with me to look over at my convenience once I reached Melrose in the next hour or so. Under the tray was the long, flowing white gown and golden head band I had worn during my one-time performance as Queen Esther, which I could tell had been placed there by my mother because of how it had been so neatly folded. As far as I knew, all these treasures had been placed in the little trunk by Mama, for she was one to always pick up after me, making sure anything that was considered a keepsake was safely stored away.

After looking over most of the items, I finally dressed myself and loaded the car. By leaving early, I knew I would have extra time to visit my favorite spots at Melrose, something I loved to do especially at this time of year. It was mid-May, but even still we had always been blessed with cool mornings for that month, something I found was good when it called for yard work like I was about to do. After arriving at our little family cemetery, I was surprised that someone else, probably Jess, had already done most of the work. Weeds had been pulled, ant beds poisoned, and the little bushes on each side neatly trimmed. All that was left to do was put flowers in the vase, which I did. There was a little bench we had placed just this past year a few steps from where the graves were, and after sitting for a while with my thoughts, I remembered the envelope I had brought and I retrieved it from my purse. The diary had a sheet of paper folded and sticking out, and after opening it, I realized it was my Big Thank You to God List — something I had started when I was ten years old. I couldn't help but laugh at some of the things I had written on there: "Caramel Fudge Ice Cream" and "Glad That General Bob Didn't Die" were two of the most humorous. After folding it back up, I then pulled from the envelope some newspaper clippings. There were several that pertained to the gunfight and capture of the outlaws that Daddy had been involved in; there was another that announced the news of his winning the senate seat. I took the time to read them all again, with my mind recalling details and pictures the newspaper had left out. The last thing was a picture that Mama must have placed in there. It was the picture taken by the *Enterprise Ledger* on the day the Boll Weevil Monument was dedicated. I remembered that day so well. My friend Professor Carver was supposed to give the dedication speech, but because of so much rain, a rail bed had been washed out and the train couldn't make it to Enterprise, so they had someone else to make the speech. Afterwards in front of the monument, a reporter asked several people to come forward for a picture. He asked for Bon Fleming, a city-council member who first concocted the idea and then covered the cost of the monument; H. M. Sessions, who had first bought the seed peanuts and financed the venture; C.W. Baston, who planted the majority of what Mr. Sessions brought back from South Carolina; and R. C. Conner, who owned the Enterprise Cotton Seed Oil Company, the man who offered contracts to every local farmer, which had made the whole venture a huge success. They were all there in the picture, standing side by side and shoulder to shoulder, with the only key person missing being me.

The monument was dedicated in December 1919 — almost thirty-three years before — but I still remembered the hurt and anger I felt from being left out of it all. It wasn't just the picture, but also the many articles that had been written over the years, each one including a quote from this person or that, but never once was my name ever mentioned. I had felt slighted by the whole affair. Here, I had prayed off and on for two years that God would raise his hand to help, and not just for those in our area, but for everyone across the South who had been struck by the boll weevil. The other thing was, I had handed off the information just like God had wanted me to do, and I had even made sure that once someone was found for the venture, the peanuts would be supplied. The way I felt at the time, I kept mostly to myself, but I did remember telling God, in my anger, that if he had something else he wanted done, he could find someone else.

Once I had looked at the pictures and realized how my thoughts still held the same bitterness, even after all this time, I felt ashamed. It also occurred to me that although I might have been slighted by one or two people by chance, I now understood at my age how those little things often happen, usually without the offender even realizing it. I could easily recall several instances of being guilty of this offense myself. With my heart now seeing these things and feeling the gentle conviction that only a loving God knows when to apply, I asked him for forgiveness. I confessed every wrong thought and attitude pertaining to the situation, including one he specifically brought back to memory, which were the words I had spoken to him, "You can find someone else next time." This, He showed me, was why my spirit had been closed off to so many things over the years and why my heart was unable to receive. Although I had started my prayer of repentance seated on the little bench, I now felt compelled to kneel before God. I did so with tears streaming down my face, and I stayed there until I was done, rising easily, now that a heavy weight had been lifted from my soul.

Afterward, I felt like a new person and cried out loud praises of joy until I reached the church, thinking that even then the rocks in the driveway would take up where I had left off. As I got out of the car, I began visiting people I had not seen in years. It was wonderful to be back at my old home church, and I relished every moment of it. Pastor Seth gave a wonderful message, and from the way he still moved around the pulpit, it would be hard to convince anyone that he was now close to eighty years old. After his sermon, we all gathered in the new fellowship hall to continue our visit and eat the fine food everyone had brought. Then just as I had finished eating, Virginia Fleming, Bon's widow, came over and sat next to me with something in a little envelope.

"Janie," she said, "I was hopin you'd be here today. I guess you may have heard that Bon passed away last year."

"Yes, I did," I replied. "I still subscribe to the paper down here, and I was so sorry to read that."

"Well, thank you, hon," she said, "but what I wanted to tell you is, I finally went through all of his things the other day and when I came across this," she said, opening the envelope, "I felt sure he would want you to have it."

She then laid out before me a copy of the program from the play *Esther,* indicating that it was the back page that she wanted me to notice. I could clearly see it was a sketch Bon had drawn of the Boll Weevil Monument.

"Oh, thank you, Virginia. How sweet," I replied. "Did Bon draw lots of these for people?"

"No, just this one. This is the one he sent to Italy showin them how he wanted the monument to look."

"Well, my goodness, Virginia," I said with confusion, "is there a special reason you think he would want me to have this?"

Virginia then looked at me as if I had uttered nothing but ignorance.

"Janie, honey," she said, sounding a little aggravated, "this is the sketch Bon made of you when you played Esther. It's where he got the idea for how he wanted the monument to look."

I sat there in complete shock, my mouth open, but I was unable to say a word.

"He never told you that, did he?" she asked.

I could only shake my head to indicate that he hadn't.

"My good Lord, girl," she said. "Bon was about to lose his mind tryin to figure out what he wanted that monument to look like, and of course, everyone he mentioned it to had plenty of suggestions, which confused him even more. I finally told him, 'Bon, let's just sit down and pray about it,' and that's exactly what we did right before walkin out the door headin to your play. It's been a long time now, but I still remember how beautiful you looked in that closing scene with the light shinin down on you. It must have hit Bon the same way as it did me, cause that's when he turned this program over," she said, pointin at it, "and started sketchin. It was a good thing you stood there for a minute, givin him a chance to really capture all the detail of the character you were playin." Then, pausing, Virginia said, "You know, Bon wasn't one to ever embarrass anybody and I never heard him tell a soul where he got the idea. I really thought you knew about him doin this, though."

"No ma'am! I had no idea," I said, "and I am so astonished right now I don't know what to say."

After that, Virginia stood, patted me on the arm, and walked away, leaving the sketch with me.

Once I was back in my car and about to leave, I sat there remembering the closing scene Virginia had talked about. It was when my student Benjamin Tyler, who played the part of Mordecai sent word to Esther regarding her part as to how their people, the Jews, would be saved by her actions. Mordecai's line was, "...for who knows that you were not chosen to be queen for such a time as this?" When these words were received by me on stage, I raised my hands toward Heaven and slightly bowed my head, just like the little angel that James had carved for me. I remembered that I stood there holding that pose for a least a good minute or so in an effort to convey the message of how Esther must have realized how God's hand had placed her in this position for a most important task, one that would save an entire race of people.

We were in such a hurry to leave once our production was over because our driver could not see well at night and had asked us to load up as soon as we were finished. That explained why Bon never approached me with what he had done that afternoon; he didn't have the chance to, and with me living away from home then and hardly ever visiting Pastor Seth's church, I'm sure he just figured we would eventually run into each other, and he'd tell me. Of course, we never did.

I remained in a state of shock while driving through town on my way home, and I could do nothing more than shake my head in awe about the whole thing. Almost thirty years ago, I was angry about being left out, and now I had just discovered that I was the inspiration behind what the monument looked like. It was something I would have never dreamed of in a million years, and I sat there humbled before my God.

There was no doubt in my mind that God had set me up for this whole thing. First, with finding the trunk and getting it open. Then seeing the picture from the newspaper clipping, which brought back the bitterness I still had in my heart over the incident, and finally, what He had hoped I would do, which was ask for His forgiveness because of what I had done. And now that I had repented, it seemed as if my eyes were opened to see and understand the spiritual implications of the position God had placed me in all those years ago. I had stood in the gap for my people and like Queen Esther, was obedient to the purpose for which I had been called. What an overwhelming sense of joy I now had for being a part of it all!

As I approached Main Street in downtown Enterprise and saw the monument, I could not help but pull aside to look it over once again. It had aged a bit in the elements and now, unlike in its beginning, held a boll weevil in her outstretched hands. There was also the dedication plaque which read:

IN PROFOUND APPRECIATION OF THE BOLL WEEVIL
AND WHAT IT HAS DONE AS THE HERALD OF PROSPERITY
THIS MONUMENT WAS ERECTED
BY THE CITIZENS OF ENTERPRISE,
COFFEE COUNTY, ALABAMA
DECEMBER 11, 1919

I knew the monument had become well known over the years, even bringing ridicule from some who were ignorant of what it truly symbolized. But to those of us who were a part of it all and held fast to its meaning, we knew that the little bug that had once eaten our cotton was much more than just a happenstance, but something that God allowed in our lives to change the road we were on. And because He did, we, the keepers of this truth, should always be blessed to tell others not to despair in their time of trouble but rather encourage them to lift their hands toward the Heavens and thank God for boll weevils.

Courtesy of Keith Ellis, Enterprise, AL

Enterprise Boll Weevil Monument

About the Author

A life-long resident of Alabama, Rhett Barbaree spent his younger years growing up in Andalusia and Mobile before moving to Clanton where he attended Chilton County High School. After graduating in 1978 he attended Troy State University. His hobbies include old west & civil war history and on occasion, a good/bad game of golf. Self employed in marketing and advertising sales he once again resides in Clanton with his wife Amy and two children, Dison and Maci.

Additional Information and Invitation

I invite you to research further on the subject of the boll weevil and the devastating effects it had on the southern United States in the early 1900's. You are also invited to attend the Boll Weevil Festivals, held twice yearly in Enterprise, Alabama and the annual Peanut Festival in Dothan, Alabama. While you are in Enterprise be sure to visit the Pea River Historical and Genealogical Society and The Depot Museum, and don't forget the very interesting George Washington Carver Museum which is on the campus of Tuskegee University in Tuskegee, Alabama.

I'd like to hear from you! Please visit my page on facebook, Thank God for Boll Weevils and also visit the website www.ThankGodforBollweevils.com. Please share these with your friends!

Finally, if God has changed your life by allowing you to walk a difficult road, I'd like to hear about and possibly use it for a future book project. Your story can revolve around many things such as a broken or restored relationship, the loss of a job, a sickness or disability, the death of a loved one, or something as simple as getting lost in the woods, which changed the outlook of your life. Please read the guidelines for Book Project Submissions on the website. Questions for discussions in small groups or for Sunday school classes can also be found at the same website.

www.ThankGodforBollWeevils.com

Questions for Further Discussion

1. Most of this book has been written in Southern dialect. Does this method of writing improve the reader's appreciation of the story or not? Why?

2. The time period of this work deals primarily with some of the most disastrous periods of Southern history: late Reconstruction; and the invasion of the boll weevil and loss of the main crop of the South, along with the displacement of thousands of people. Yet the story is surprisingly warm and humorous. How does the author achieve this mood in spite of all that is happening in the story?

3. Does the author develop his central characters well? Do you want to know more about them?

4. Daddy Jack plays a significant role within the book. Yet during most of the work, he has already died. How does the author succeed with this somber character?

5. Is Pastor Seth believable? He seems to be the catalyst for much of the story's action. How does Barbaree accomplish this?

6. What does the Boll Weevil statue symbolize?

7. George Washinghton Carver played an important role to the continuing success of the economy in the South. In what way was this accomplished? Did you like the way his character was presented in the book?

8. Most sharecroppers during this period were illiterate and lacked the opportunity for an education. When Janie's mother offered them a chance to attend school, was it believable to you as the reader?

9. During the early 1900's there were still many living who had some experiences from the Civil War. Did the book convey enough of its history to give you an idea of what the South's sentiment was towards the North at this time?

10. If you had to choose, who was your favorite character in the book? Why?

11. The story is a fiction based on true events. Does that intrigue you to research the facts of what really happened?

12. Out of the over three hundred uses Professor Carver created for the peanut, you can still find many of them being packaged and sold through your local grocery store. Were you aware of the longevity of his research? Can you name a few of these products?

13. Janie realized a new symbolic gesture for the boll weevil monument at the end of the story. Do you agree with it? Would you change the ending? If so how?

Acknowledgments

During this past year, there have been several people who have patiently listened to or read my story chapter by chapter as I was writing it. My wife Amy is one of those whom I could never thank enough for her opinions and insight. To Louise and Mike Staman of Tiger Iron Press, I will be forever indebted for the opportunity that only a few new authors enjoy. To my front line editor, Van English, who worked diligently to correct and polish my manuscript and Karen Staman who showed me how and where to put the icing on the cake. To my mother Lana and my brother Robin, as well as other family members and countless friends who have all had a hand in one way or another throughout its entirety, you are blessings; and to my precious children Dison and Maci, who have encouraged me by simply asking questions or acting excited about what I was doing, you inspire me; and finally, to you, my reader, I owe the greatest appreciation of all. God bless!